The Grace Message

THE
GRACE
MESSAGE

Is the Gospel really this good?

Andrew Farley

Foreword by Bart Millard of MercyMe

SALEM
BOOKS

an imprint of Regnery Publishing
Washington, D.C.

The author is represented by Don Gates at The Gates Group, www.the-gates-group.com.

Salem Books™ is a trademark of Salem Communications Holding Corporation

Regnery® is a registered trademark and its colophon is a trademark of Salem Communications Holding Corporation

Cataloging-in-Publication data on file with the Library of Congress

ISBN: 978-1-68451-128-0
eISBN: 978-1-68451-287-4

Library of Congress Control Number: 2021946355

Published in the United States by
Salem Books
An Imprint of Regnery Publishing
A Division of Salem Media Group
Washington, D.C.
www.SalemBooks.com

Manufactured in the United States of America

10 9 8 7 6 5 4 3 2 1

Books are available in quantity for promotional or premium use. For information on discounts and terms, please visit our website: www.SalemBooks.com.

This book is dedicated to our faithful supporters

and our devoted team at AndrewFarley.org.

CONTENTS

FOREWORD

I came to Christ when I was thirteen years old, but I always felt like something was missing. Then, fast-forward decades later to my first encounter with the grace message.

It's hard to believe the religious ideas you've been told your entire life aren't quite the whole truth. So, at first, the grace message seemed too good to be true. But all of a sudden, the light turns on and you go free in the finished work of Christ. The powerful simplicity of the message just blows you away!

In no uncertain terms, Andrew Farley shows why the good news is actually great news. This extraordinary, battle-tested message of hope and freedom has a proven track record of transforming lives. And it's a surprising alternative to the popular behavior-improvement message that offers no more than the illusion of sin management. There's just no comparison, so don't settle for less.

The Grace Message is bursting with truth. The love of God practically drips from its pages. God can use this important book to reinvigorate your faith as you discover how to get way more out of your new life in Christ. Here, you'll celebrate Jesus to the fullest and maybe even fall in love with Him all over again. Read it and see for yourself!

Bart Millard
singer/songwriter for MercyMe

DANGEROUS GRACE

A few years ago, I was giving a weekend conference on the grace message. There were a few hundred people packed into the fellowship hall of a small church in the Midwest. Some were taking notes, and many were asking questions.

Everyone was loving it. Well, *almost* everyone.

I could tell one man was really struggling with what I was saying. He couldn't reconcile everything he was hearing with what he'd been taught his whole life. Halfway through the second day, he hit his breaking point. He jumped to his feet in the middle of the session and, in a belligerent tone, declared, "All you talk about is grace. What about the deeper things of the Gospel?

"You're ignoring the sanctification process," he continued. "Yes, we're saved by grace, but you preach a message of cheap grace. You're giving people a license to sin!"

"A license to sin?" I questioned. "People seem to be sinning just fine without a license. What if we give God's grace a chance?"

He stormed out of the room, leaving the audience wondering what might happen next.

This wasn't the first time someone got revved up enough to speak out during my teaching. And it certainly wouldn't be the last. Over the years, I've seen people become furious and walk out of Bible studies, conference sessions, and Sunday morning services—all because they didn't agree that God's grace was really *this* good.

The fact is that many people—yes, even lots of well-intentioned believers in Jesus—object to a focus on God's grace. To them, too much grace seems dangerous. Maybe they think grace teachers are secretly leading lives of wild, unrestrained sin and leading others down that road too. So they attack the message, calling it "cheap grace" or "greasy grace" or "hyper-grace."

The Truth about Grace

Cheap grace? It cost Jesus everything, and it's absolutely *free* to us! Greasy grace? We're not climbing a firepole up to God and slipping back. God climbed down to us in the person of Christ. Hyper-grace? Well, I'm certainly hyper about God's never-ending grace. Aren't you? The Bible actually uses the expression "hyper" to describe God's grace:

Romans 5:20: *hypereperisseusen*—God's grace over-abounded!

Ephesians 2:7: *hyperballon*—God's grace surpasses and exceeds (expectations)!

1 Timothy 1:14: *hyperepleonasen*—God's grace was in surpassing abundance!

The Greek prefix *hyper*, meaning "above and beyond," "over the top," or "in excess," is used a few times to describe God's grace in the New Testament. Why shouldn't we be "hyper" about the surpassing overabundance of His grace?

- God is the God of all grace (1 Peter 5:10).
- Grace is multiplied to us in the knowledge of Him (2 Peter 1:2).
- Jesus is full of grace (John 1:14).
- The Old Testament prophesied about this grace we have today (1 Peter 1:10).
- There's more than enough grace to go around (1 Timothy 1:14).
- We've received an abundance of grace (Romans 5:17).
- For us, it's "grace upon grace" (John 1:16).
- We stand in grace (Romans 5:2).
- The grace of God overflows to us (Romans 5:15).
- The Gospel itself is called the "gospel of grace" (Acts 20:24; Galatians 1:6).
- We're saved by grace (Ephesians 2:5, 8).
- Grace doesn't just bring salvation. It teaches us to say "no" to sin (Titus 2:11–12).
- It's important not to miss the grace of God (Hebrews 12:15).

- When there's sinning going on, God dishes out grace even more (Romans 5:20; Romans 6:1).
- God knows sin won't master us if we're under His grace (Romans 6:14).
- Paul and Barnabas urged converts to continue in God's grace (Acts 13:43).
- We're supposed to set our hope completely on God's grace (1 Peter 1:13).
- It's good for our hearts to be strengthened by grace (Hebrews 13:9).
- We grow in grace (2 Peter 3:18).
- We're called to stand firm and be strong in the grace of God (1 Peter 5:12; 2 Timothy 2:1).

I could keep going.

Is too much grace dangerous? Only to the enemy! For us, it seems God's grace is not only safe but essential. You really don't have to worry about "too much grace." Paul says it's foolish to start by the grace of God and continue any other way (Galatians 3:1–3; Colossians 2:6–7).

No Deeper Message

There's a terribly erroneous idea in the Church today that God's grace is only "cookies and candy" and that we need to focus on the "deeper" message of "stop your sinning." That's the core problem in the Church today: Those who think "stop sinning" is a deeper message can find that anywhere—from the message of John the Baptist to many world religions. In reality, there is no deeper message than "the gospel of grace" (Acts 20:24). We never graduate from God's grace!

However, many people sitting in our churches today are getting a lightweight understanding of God's grace. They think it's merely about forgiveness when they fail and Heaven when they die. They don't see the empowerment of God's grace, so they seek to lessen it, temper it, or balance it with something else. They kill their victory over sin and don't even realize it:

> **For sin shall no longer be your master**, *because you are not under the law, but* **under grace**. (Romans 6:14)

Grace isn't just the treatment for sin; it's the cure. More grace means more victory over sin. Less grace means less victory over sin. Do we really want *less* victory? If so, less grace is the sure way to get there.

The Grace Message

Grace is a word we all know, yet we so often fail to really believe in what it means. Grace is both essential and dazzling. It raises eyebrows. It begs questions. Grace turns everything upside down.

In this book, I invite you to get in on the best flavor of Christianity and celebrate the good news of the Gospel like never before. It will awaken you to a revolutionary perspective every healthy Christian should have.

Life is too short to miss out on God's best, and what you don't know about God's grace can hinder you from experiencing the joy of Jesus in every area of your life. So if you've been weighed down by ruthless religion, or if you've been searching for that high-octane version of the Gospel that you know must exist, this is it.

Get ready to be boosted into a remarkable new confidence. Here, you'll be challenged to dismiss the lies you've believed and make up your own mind about how big God's grace really is.

Welcome to *The Grace Message*.

PART 1

FLIRTING WITH MOSES

CHAPTER 1

Eric was frustrated. He couldn't understand how anyone would be motivated to live a godly life if God's grace was as big as I was claiming. He called in to our radio program to voice his objection.

"If I believe what you're saying, then what's my incentive to not lay around and smoke weed all day?"

"Is that what you want, Eric? To lay around and smoke weed?" I asked.

"No! I don't want that," he exclaimed. "I'm just saying, what's the incentive for someone to want to do good if they've already got the golden ticket to Heaven?"

"It doesn't sound like you need an incentive, Eric," I said. "You already indicated you don't want to do those things."

"I'm not talking about me," he replied scornfully. "I'm talking about *other* believers."

Eric's concern is not uncommon. I hear it all the time.

People are afraid of too much grace—not for themselves, but for "those other people over there." They're scared other believers will just go out and do whatever they want.

They're scared of what Christians *want*.

But God took out our stony hearts and gave us new, obedient hearts (Romans 6:17). He promised to work in us to cause us to want what He wants (Philippians 2:13). Apparently, God isn't afraid of what believers really want!

God can afford to put us under grace with no limits, because His grace doesn't stop at forgiveness. He also gives us new spiritual passions and desires. The Bible says we're now allergic to sin and addicted to Jesus (Romans 6:11).

You're Safe under Grace

I'm allergic to eggs. They're a real shock to my system. My body rejects them, and when I slip, all kinds of alarming symptoms warn me of what I've eaten and how profoundly it disagrees with me. In the same way, sin is a real shock to your system. Your new identity in Christ rejects sin. All kinds of alarms go off when you sin. It's "all hands on deck" to resolve the situation.

You're allergic to sin and addicted to Jesus. You may *think* you want to sin. You may *feel* like you want to sin. But you're going to prove your new identity one way or another: by sinning and being miserable or by expressing Jesus and being fulfilled. Either way, you prove you're a slave of righteousness (Romans 6:18). You can't escape your destiny of displaying

Christ. You're fused to Him, bonded to Him forever. You can't get away from your new core desires.

When we're worried about too much grace, it's because our view of grace is puny and pitiful. Some see grace simply as mercy for when we fail, or a ticket to Heaven, or God canceling our debt. Sure, those things are a *part* of God's grace, but let's not settle for anything less than the fullness of God's grace. In His grace, God took a spiritual scalpel and cut out your sinful heart and replaced it with a beautiful, new heart that always loves Jesus. That's part of what God's grace did too.

Grace is more than mercy, more than forgiveness, more than a ticket to Heaven. Is God's grace a "get out of jail free" card? Yes, and it's also a "get a new heart for free" card. We believers should be celebrating *both*.

That's where we find true balance as God intended. Instead of pumping the brakes on how big God's love and grace are, we should simply be adding the message of new identity and new desire into the mix. We have every reason to push the accelerator to the floor when it comes to grace!

You've already been doing what you *think* you want to do, and so far there's been no lightning strike. What if you started doing what you *actually* want and allowed the freeing atmosphere of God's grace to help you discover your truest desires?

When the sky's the limit, what do you really want? Have you noticed that when you sin, it never really pays off? *Sinning is the best way to be miserable.* And living under grace—with a new and better option—makes you realize this more quickly.

Let's Get Specific!

Without a good understanding of the Gospel, grace can feel nebulous. The Gospel shows you God's grace in specific ways. It allows you to define God's grace with precision. Without it, you're left with whatever you might think God feels toward you.

There are lots of teachings out there that claim God is good and God is gracious. But the Gospel gets down to pinpoint accuracy about God's grace. This means you no longer have to constantly wonder: *How forgiven am I? How secure am I? How new am I?* Through the Gospel, God gives you specific (and exhilarating!) answers.

Attempts to throw stones at God's grace usually start with the premise that it is nothing more than mercy or forgiveness when we've fallen. But God's grace is actually empowering. Crying "too much grace" is like complaining about "too much victory over sin." By God's grace, we've been given righteousness and new life and new desires. God's grace is a dynamic force at work in our lives every moment as He teaches us to say "no" to sin and "yes" to who we really are in Christ (Titus 2:11–12).

So, are you ready to set aside Law-based living and trust God's grace all the way?

> *The former regulation is **set aside** because it was **weak** and **useless** (for the law made nothing perfect), and **a better hope** is introduced, by which we **draw near** to God.* (Hebrews 7:18–19)

CHAPTER 2

Our Sunday service had just finished, and I was standing at the door greeting people on their way out. A woman came up and introduced herself—an older woman named Evelyn. She'd attended our church a few times, she said, and each time she'd heard something that made her come back for more. Today, she'd gathered up her courage to talk to me about it.

"I've been a Christian all my life. I'm now almost seventy years old," she said. "All that time in church, though, and I never heard much about the New Covenant. But you're putting into words what I always knew was true in my heart. I wish I had heard this forty years ago!"

Sadly, the New Covenant (the New Testament message of God's grace) goes mostly unaddressed in the Christian world today. Think about it: How many sermons have you heard in your lifetime that highlighted what the New Covenant is and why it is so much better than the Old Covenant?

I've heard that Hebrews is the least-studied epistle in the New Testament, yet it's the one that brags the most about all we enjoy in the New Covenant. For many Christians, the term "New Covenant" is just the name of a church down the street. You know, New Covenant Bible Church or New Covenant Chapel of God.

So, what's the New Covenant really all about? Well, at salvation, we enter into a contract of sorts, but it's not a contract of our own making. The New Covenant is *nothing like* the "we will obey everything" promise that Israel made at the foot of Mount Sinai (Exodus 24:7).

This New Covenant is totally different ... on purpose. Why? Because Old Testament followers could *not* remain faithful. This is why the writer of Hebrews, quoting extensively from the Old Testament book of Jeremiah, says:

> But **God found fault with the people** and said: *"The days are coming, declares the Lord, when I will make a new covenant with the people of Israel and with the people of Judah.* **It will not be like the covenant I made with their ancestors** *when I took them by the hand to lead them out of Egypt,* **because they did not remain faithful to my covenant,** *and I turned away from them, declares the Lord.*
>
> *"This is the covenant I will establish with the people of Israel after that time, declares the Lord.* **I will put my laws in their minds and write them on their hearts. I will be their God, and they will be my people.**

*"No longer will they teach their neighbor, or say to one another, 'Know the Lord,' because **they will all know me, from the least of them to the greatest. For I will forgive their wickedness and will remember their sins no more.**"* (Hebrews 8:8–12)

Hebrews announces the New Covenant is radically different from the Old. The number one reason for this is that the Israelites couldn't remain obedient to God's law. They were unfaithful.

So what does God do differently in this New Covenant? He rigs everything. Through Jesus, we are God's people, no matter what. We know Him intuitively. He put His desires inside us. Now we want what He wants. Our sin record is gone forever. God's not keeping score with us. In short, the New Covenant is a download (of a new heart) and a deletion (of your sins).

A Broken Promise

"When I was in college, I promised God I would go into full-time ministry, and I never did," William confessed. "I still look back and wonder if I let Him down, and if I'm even saved. If I am still saved, I feel like a total failure for not keeping my promise to Him. Now everything feels like God's second best in my life."

I felt terrible for him. William hung his head as he spoke and couldn't even look me in the eye. It was clear that this was the source of a deep and abiding sense of failure and shame in his life. It had taken a lot of courage for him to approach me about this. Thankfully, I had an idea.

"What if God never asked you to make Him that promise in the first place?" I suggested.

"What do you mean?" William asked, confused. He'd never considered his problem from this angle before.

"Well, we humans are horrible promise keepers. It's not just you. All of us are," I explained. "That's why the New Covenant is not about us keeping promises to God. It's about God's big promise to Himself."

As I began to share the truth about Jesus's being the ultimate Promise Keeper, I could see William start to relax inside. There was hope. Maybe he didn't have to continue to see himself as a failure. Maybe he could focus on God's promises to him, rather than his promises to God.

And this opened the door to an even more revolutionary thought: What if God never held any expectations over him to begin with?

Another Broken Promise

How are you at promise-keeping? How about keeping New Year's resolutions? If you're like me, you've broken a few promises over the years, and you've failed to keep up your end of the bargain at least a time or two.

The Israelites were no different when it came to promise-keeping. They weren't good at it at all. Here in Exodus 24, we see how they promised to keep the whole Law:

> When Moses went and told the people all the Lord's words and laws, they responded with one voice, "**Everything the Lord has said we will do.**" . . . Then he took

*the Book of the Covenant and read it to the people. They
responded, "**We will do everything the Lord has said;
we will obey.**" (Exodus 24:37)*

There were 613 commands in the Law. Some of them car-
ried a punishment of death for non-compliance. So Israel was
making quite a promise!

How did it go for them? If you're familiar with the Old
Testament, you know it's a story of failure upon failure and
promises to rededicate and do better, followed by even more
failure. Perhaps the whole experience is best summarized here
in Psalm 78:

*But they put God to the test and rebelled against the
Most High; **they did not keep his statutes**. Like their
ancestors they were **disloyal** and **faithless**, as **unreliable**
as a faulty bow. They angered him with their high places;
they aroused his jealousy with their idols. When God
heard them, he was furious; **he rejected Israel completely**. (Psalm 78:56–59)*

Ouch! And it wasn't just the common people of Israel
who were failing. The priests who were leading the nation
were just as bad at keeping promises. Here's what God said
about them:

*"And now, **you priests**, this warning is for you. If you
do not listen, and if you do not resolve to honor my
name," says the Lord Almighty, "I will send a curse on
you, and I will curse your blessings. Yes, I have already*

*cursed them, because **you have not resolved to honor me**."* (Malachi 2:1–2)

Apparently, nobody could keep their promises to God. And maybe that was the whole point. The first promise-keepers convention was a failure. Plus, Israel's initial disobedience was only a preview of coming attractions. Therefore, God decided to usher in something new and different through Jesus. This New Covenant would not be about our promise-keeping. No, it would be about God's promise-keeping to Himself:

> *Because God wanted to make the **unchanging nature of his purpose** very clear to the heirs of what was promised, he confirmed it with an oath. God did this so that, **by two unchangeable things in which it is impossible for God to lie**, we who have fled to take hold of the hope set before us may be greatly encouraged. We have this hope as **an anchor for the soul**, firm and secure.* (Hebrews 6:17–19a)

What anchors us today is not our promises to God but His promise to Himself! Yes, two unchangeable things (God and God) are what sustain us. It's impossible for God to lie, right? So a truth-telling God on one side and a truth-telling God on the other side secure us as saved people forever. God Himself is our anchor. God is the only true Promise Keeper.

*When God made his promise to Abraham, since there was no one greater for him to swear by, **he swore by himself.*** (Hebrews 6:13)

CHAPTER 3

I was flipping through TV stations late one night after watching a basketball game. A mention of King David caught my attention, so I paused on the preaching channel for a few minutes.

"David had such an amazing walk with God. Would you like that kind of walk?" the well-known evangelist asked temptingly. The Bible calls King David "a man after God's own heart," after all. Who wouldn't like to be called that too?

The preacher continued, "You can begin the journey toward the intimacy with God that David enjoyed by praying through Psalm 139 and asking God to reveal the sin in your heart." That's where things came to a screeching halt. It was a formula I'd heard many times before.

Perhaps you have too. First, you're told to consider your favorite Old Testament hero of the faith. Would it be Samson, or Esther, or Solomon? Then, you're asked if you'd like to have the relationship with God they enjoyed—and of course, who wouldn't? Finally, you're given the formula for how you can get there. And where does that formula begin? With your effort as you attempt to get your heart right, cleanse yourself of sin, do more, and be more for God.

Now I'm going to say something surprising. Would I want what Old Testament believers had? Would I want God to view me the way He viewed David, or Esther, or Hosea?

No, I wouldn't.

You heard that right: I really wouldn't. Why not? Because we have something better than anything anyone experienced in the Old Testament.

> *Some faced jeers and flogging, and even chains and imprisonment. They were put to death by stoning; they were sawed in two; they were killed by the sword. They went about in sheepskins and goatskins, destitute, persecuted and mistreated—the world was not worthy of them. They wandered in deserts and mountains, living in caves and in holes in the ground. These were all commended for their faith, **yet none of them received what had been promised, since God had planned something better for us so that only together with us would they be made perfect.** (Hebrews 11:36–40)*

They were flogged, put in chains, imprisoned, stoned to death, sawn in two, and killed with swords. Dedicated? Absolutely. Committed? For sure. Sold out? All the way! Yet they did not receive what was promised. And you have something better today because *you live on this side of the cross.*

A Better Covenant

What exactly is better for you today? In short, *everything.* We'll get into it all soon, but here are some starters:

- Under the Old Covenant, God was angry with Israel about sins. Under the New, you've been saved from the wrath of God (Romans 5:9).
- Under the Old, animal sacrifices were yearly reminders of sins. Under the New, God remembers your sins no more (Hebrews 8:12).
- Under the Old, the Holy Spirit would come upon people temporarily for divine acts of service. Under the New, the Holy Spirit is sealed in you forever (Ephesians 1:13–14).
- Under the Old, David pleaded, "Do not cast me from your presence or take your Holy Spirit from me" (Psalm 51:11). Under the New, you are one spirit with the Lord (1 Corinthians 6:17), and He'll never leave you (Hebrews 13:5).

Christ is the mediator of the New Covenant (Hebrews 9:15), and this new way of grace is much better than the old way of law.

*But in fact the ministry Jesus has received is as **superior** to theirs as the covenant of which he is mediator is*

superior to the old one, since the new covenant is estab-
lished on *better promises*. (Hebrews 8:6)

The Salvation Guarantee

I receive a lot of emails from people who have questions.
On many days, I answer dozens asking for clarification on a
point of doctrine or something they've heard in church. Many
times, they are cries for help from people who've already been
searching for answers and haven't been able to find them
anywhere.

"I'm having panic attacks all the time, and I can't see any
way out," one late-night email began. "Growing up, my parents taught me I could lose my salvation if my heart turned
away from God.

"I've struggled with this my whole Christian life," the
emailer continued, "and I feel like I'm at the end of my rope.
Have I turned away from Him? I've been unfaithful to God
so many times, I don't know where I stand or if I'm even saved
anymore."

Sadly, this email is not unusual. I've received many others
just like it. And this may resonate with you too. You might
worry about whether your salvation is secure. You may have
wondered what might happen if you were to commit a *really*
big sin. Or what if you fall into severe struggle or even addiction and commit very frequent sins? Will these somehow
cancel the contract you have with God?

No, they won't—because they can't.

Remember that God never asked for your faithfulness as
the way to keep your salvation. We hear people today saying,

"I swear on the Bible" or "I swear on my mother's grave!" They seek to swear by something greater than themselves, but there's no one greater than God. That's why He swore by Himself (Hebrews 6:13). The result is that you are incredibly secure in your salvation. Jesus is your guarantee, and there's no fine print in the contract to worry about.

You may ask, "But what if I sin a lot?" or "But what if I commit the same sin over and over?" You wonder when you might breach the contract, ruin the deal, or kill the covenant. But you're not in the equation. As we saw already, on one side of the contract, you've got the God of the Universe, who is no liar. On the other side, you've got the same truth-telling, promise-keeping God holding everything up.

> *... because of this oath,* **Jesus has become the guarantor** *of a better covenant.* (Hebrews 7:22)

This New Covenant is *not* about you and your dedication, your commitment, or your faithfulness. It's actually about God's faithfulness to Himself. That's what secures you.

You enjoy a covenant that you didn't initiate and that you don't maintain or sustain. God wants you to celebrate your security. So go ahead: Brag on Jesus and all He accomplished for you!

Because He Lives

Most who believe salvation is something that can be lost have a habit of mentally showcasing their sins front and center. They imagine that what they do ruins their salvation. In so doing, they mistake the New Covenant for the Old Covenant. Under the New Covenant, your salvation depends not on how you are living but on *how long Jesus lives*:

> ... but **because Jesus lives forever,** he has a permanent priesthood. Therefore he is able to save completely those who come to God through him, **because he always lives** to intercede for them. (Hebrews 7:24–25)

Because Jesus lives forever, you're saved forever. It's not about the duration of your faithfulness, it's about the longevity of Christ's life. You'll be saved as long as Jesus lives.

And that's forever!

Faithfulness was an Old Covenant problem solved by the New. Christ lives in us always. He'll never disown Himself, so He'll never disown you.

> If we are faithless, **he remains faithful,** for he **cannot disown himself.** (2 Timothy 2:13)

CHAPTER 4

For some people, life just seems to start off on the right foot. That was the case for Lisa.

"As a teen, I was popular and successful in school," she told me. "I enjoyed going to church and seeing my friends, and I wasn't really worried about anything. Life seemed good, and I was confident that God loved me."

Then things started to go downhill. "My younger brother got seriously ill," she said, "and that seemed to set off a whole chain of events. My parents started fighting with each other, all the money we had was going to medical bills. They didn't have time to talk to me anymore; I didn't even want to come home after school." Lisa paused there, struggling with her memories. Eventually, she continued.

"To fill the void, I turned to boys, partying, and ultimately that led to anorexia," she confessed. "At that point, my parents realized something was wrong and took me to a psychiatrist, but I never could find something that filled the void. So, I turned to church on my own—I started going to a church that emphasized obedience to Old Testament rules. It seems like I went down the aisle every time there was an altar call. I tried practicing their spiritual disciplines and even joined an accountability group. But the harder I tried, the more hopeless I felt. My obedience was never enough. It wasn't until I stumbled upon your ministry that I found real acceptance in Jesus, and I realized what I'd been searching for all along."

Lisa's experience is what happens to anyone who truly takes a stab at Old Testament Law or rule-keeping. Let's face it: Israel was pretty bad at Law-keeping, and so is anyone today who tries to keep the Law. What's ironic is that God never gave the Law with the expectation that it would make people righteous anyway:

> *For if a law had been given that could impart life, then **righteousness** would certainly have come by the law.* (Galatians 3:21b)

The Law Is Not of Faith

The Law could never impart life. And righteousness was never intended to come by the Law. After a lifelong study of the Jewish Law, the Apostle Paul came to this conclusion:

> *[We] know that a person is **not justified by the works of the law**, but by faith in Jesus Christ. So we, too, have put our faith in Christ Jesus that we may be*

*justified by faith in Christ and **not by the works of the law**, because by the works of the law **no one** will be justified.* (Galatians 2:16)

Nobody is made right by the works of the Law—not one single person. It's only by faith in Jesus Christ that you're justified before God. The Law is not based on faith:

*Clearly no one who relies on the law is justified before God, because "the righteous will live by faith." **The law is not based on faith**; on the contrary, it says, "The person who does these things will live by them."* (Galatians 3:11–12)

Eternal life only comes by faith. It takes no faith at all to simply obey some rules and regulations from the Law. No one can keep the Law, and no one can obtain eternal life through the Law either.

This is not some new teaching or new conclusion we arrive at today. Rightness with God has always been by faith, not by religious works—even in the Old Testament. Abraham is a perfect example of this:

*It was **not through the law that Abraham** and his offspring received the promise that he would be heir of the world, **but through the righteousness that comes by faith**.* (Romans 4:13)

Abraham was made right with God long before the Law was even given. And he serves as a beautiful example of what it means to be in perfect standing with God apart from any human effort or law-keeping. Abraham was made right by faith alone, and so are you!

A Deal Is a Deal

Imagine sitting in the home you've owned for 430 days. Then you receive a phone call from the seller asking you for more money. More money? It's not happening, right? A deal is a deal, and there's no way you're going back and renegotiating a contract that was already signed and ratified 430 days ago.

Likewise, the promise of the New Covenant given to Abraham is older even than the Old Covenant. That's right: In one sense, the New is older than the Old. The way of faith predates the way of law.

> *The law, introduced 430 years later, does not set aside the covenant previously established by God and thus do away with the promise.* (Galatians 3:17b)

Moses came down Mount Sinai with those tablets in hand about 430 years after Abraham was given the promise of righteousness by faith. This 430-year separation helps us differentiate faith and the Law. The Law is not of faith (Galatians 3:12). That's right, faith and the Law are separate systems, and never the two shall meet. The Law's arrival didn't change God's promise: A deal is a deal!

And when you realize that God approves of you—apart from anything you do—it changes everything. You begin to view yourself and God in light of what Jesus did for you rather than what you try to do for Him.

The Passport of Jesus

My wife loves researching our family tree. She finds it fascinating to learn of our lineage, heritage, and history. From her research she's discovered, for example, that one of her many-times great-grandfathers was the next-door neighbor to Benedict Arnold, and one of mine was Robert the Bruce. She also figured out that one family in our church who have the same last name as my mother are in fact my ninth cousins. And she found a journal that her eighth great-grandfather, a traveling preacher from Rhode Island, wrote in the 1700s.

How does this relate to Jesus Christ and the Law? Interestingly, one of the strongest arguments for abandoning Law-based living and celebrating the New Covenant relates to the ancestry of Jesus—His lineage.

For thousands of years, only members of the tribe of Levi could serve as high priests in Israel. Absolutely zero people from the tribe of Judah ever served:

> *He of whom these things are said belonged to a different tribe, and **no one from that tribe has ever served at the altar**. For it is clear that our Lord descended from **Judah**, and in regard to that tribe Moses said **nothing** about priests.* (Hebrews 7:13–14)

So here comes Jesus, from the tribe of Judah, now serving as our High Priest. According to the Law, He's disqualified to serve in that capacity. He has the wrong paperwork, the wrong lineage, the wrong heritage.

Why did God do this? What's He trying to tell you? You call upon Jesus from the tribe of Judah to save you. So, you can't call upon Him and then look to the Law to keep you saved or grow you. That's a total contradiction. The Law says Jesus can't serve as priest!

So, what's the solution? If you're changing the priesthood, you simply need to be consistent and change the Law too:

> For when **the priesthood** is changed, **the law** must be changed also. (Hebrews 7:12)

There's no better argument than the lineage of Jesus for abandoning the Law and looking to God's New Covenant of grace. That's because a change of priesthood (from Levi to Judah) requires a change of covenant (from Old to New). A change of priesthood means a change of Law.

So, here's Jesus, from the tribe of Judah, breaking all the rules, and that's the whole point. We've got a new kind of priest to go with our New Covenant. You don't put new wine into old wineskins (Matthew 9:17). It's out with the Old and in with the New!

CHAPTER 5

I have a lot of conversations at the door of the church. One Sunday morning, I was standing there as people were walking out after the service when Kyle came up and asked if he could talk to me for a minute. He looked worried. Since there was an empty office behind us, I stepped back, opened the door, and motioned him in.

"What's on your mind?" I asked.

"Well, I did appreciate what you had to say this morning," Kyle said—but he looked concerned. "I grew up in a denomination that mixed law and grace. I went to our Bible school and became a pastor within our movement. For years, I preached 'Christian law'—a series of dos and don'ts—without a second thought," he explained.

"In the back of my mind, though, I knew something was wrong. I wasn't keeping the laws I was teaching my own

congregation, and I wasn't close to living the way I was asking
them to live. I eventually quit the ministry, and it wasn't until
years later that I really came to understand God's grace. Now,
I wish I could go back and re-preach all those sermons!"

He looked discouraged and frustrated. And that made
sense: He probably felt as if he'd wasted so many years and
not only his time, but others' as well.

"Well, here's the thing," I said. "God has a way of still
ministering to people despite our faults and misunderstand-
ings. Plus, it's not too late. God is always on time. We're
forgiven for all our mistakes, and you're now coming to know
God's grace on just the right schedule. God knew this would
happen, even if you didn't."

Perhaps you can relate to Kyle's concern in one way or
another. Maybe you wish you could've understood God's
grace better from the very beginning. Let me encourage you
that, like Kyle, you're right on schedule. God is showing you
the impossibility of law and the beauty of grace. It's never too
late to shift your thinking on this.

Seeking Clarity

There's nothing wrong with the Law itself. It's holy, righteous, and good (Romans 7:12). The problem lies with the
people under the Law.

> For if there had been nothing wrong with that first cove-
> nant, no place would have been sought for another. **But
> God found fault with the people.**... (Hebrews 8:7–8a)

Why did God find fault with the people under the Law? Because literally no one could keep it. After all, it's not the hearers of the Law but *the doers* of the Law who are right with God:

> For it is **not those who hear the law** *who are righteous in God's sight, but it is* **those who obey the law** *who will be declared righteous.* (Romans 2:13)

This leads us to an important question: How many doers of the Law are there? The answer to that question is *zero*. There are exactly zero Law-keepers. The purpose of the Law was *never* to pat Israel on the back for the great job they were doing:

> *Now we know that whatever the law says, it says to those who are under the law, so that* **every mouth** *may be silenced and the whole world held* **accountable to God.** *Therefore* **no one** *will be declared righteous in God's sight by the works of the law; rather, through the law* **we become conscious of our sin.** (Romans 3:19–20)

The Mirror of the Law

The Law was designed to silence everyone. What can you say in response when it points out you're a sinner?

See, the Law is like a mirror. It makes us conscious of our sin problem. It helps us realize we're accountable to God. Only then can we see our need for a solution.

Even the most learned "experts" in the Law couldn't obey it. Apparently, they weren't even close!

> *For I tell you that **unless your righteousness surpasses** that of the Pharisees and the teachers of the law, you will certainly not enter the kingdom of heaven.* (Matthew 5:20)

In fact, the teachers of the Law were more hypocritical than anyone else:

> *You, then, who teach others, do you not teach yourself? You who preach against stealing, do you steal? You who say that people should not commit adultery, do you commit adultery? You who abhor idols, do you rob temples?* ***You who boast in the law, do you dishonor God by breaking the law? As it is written: "God's name is blasphemed among the Gentiles because of you."*** (Romans 2:21–24)

The Law is a dead-end street. It points out humanity's sin addiction and hypocrisy. God designed the Law to expose our problem so we'd look for a solution in Jesus.

> *Before the coming of this faith, we were held in custody under the law, locked up until the faith that was to come would be revealed.* ***So, the law was our guardian until Christ came that we might be justified by faith.*** *Now that this faith has come, we are no longer under a guardian.* (Galatians 3:23–25)

It's no fun to be held in custody, locked up in a jail cell. But that's exactly what the Law did. It locked you up until you could see your need for faith in Christ. Now that you have faith in Him, you're no longer under the guardianship of the Law. The Law has done its work in revealing your need, and your relationship with the Law is over.

Objection!

The first line of the email didn't mince any words. "You're dishonoring God's law and promoting nothing but lazy Christians who won't serve the Lord," it blasted. And it didn't get any better from there.

People have a hard time imagining how we're going to turn out okay without Moses. They'd rather Christians exert incredible effort to keep the Law when the truth is we can expect more struggle with sin, not less, under the Law.

If being under the Law is our problem, then what's the solution? At salvation, we *die* to the Law:

> *So, my brothers and sisters, you also **died to the law** through the body of Christ, that you might belong to another, to him who was raised from the dead, in order that we might **bear fruit for God**.* (Romans 7:4)

> *But now, **by dying to what once bound us**, we have been released from the law so that **we serve** in the new way of the Spirit, and not in the old way of the written code.* (Romans 7:6)

If you're all about bearing fruit and serving, there's only one way for that to happen. God wants you free from the Law so that you're trusting His life in you.

The Law is not your source, and the Law is not your goal. Knowing Jesus is your source for godly living. Knowing Jesus is the goal of the Christian life. You've died to the Law so that you can now live for God.

CHAPTER 6

Mariana looked beaten-down and depressed. I could tell by how she stood, her shoulders sagging and a hopeless look in her eyes. She was telling me about her church experiences over the years.

"I felt strangled," she explained. "It was like I was on a performance treadmill and it wouldn't ever slow down—it just sped up. It seemed like the more I tried to obey all the 'rules', the more I sinned. I was always trying harder and harder to get in God's favor, but that just made my failures bigger and bigger, and the result was guilt every time."

When she turned to people at church, she said, she kept hearing more demands—go to church, have a quiet time, join a small group, volunteer in the nursery, rededicate your life, serve, serve, serve. Everything was about doing more, and it was never enough.

Mariana continued to describe her experience in different churches (one even sounded like a cult!) where law-like demands were the norm and she felt like she could never measure up. So finally, she just quit. But she didn't know where to go from there.

I want to share with you some of what I shared with Mariana. It enabled her to understand her own experience better. It also helped her see the way to freedom. My prayer is that it encourages you too!

Professor Perfect

Imagine living with a perfectionist who has you under incredible demands. You can never do it right. If you make just one mistake, you're treated like you've done nothing good at all. But there's always the mirage of better status over the next ridge.

That's what it's like to be under the Law. The Law is an all-or-nothing proposition. The only acceptable standard is perfection:

> *For whoever keeps the whole law and yet stumbles at just **one point** is guilty of breaking **all** of it.* (James 2:10)

Under the Law, your two possible scores are 0 and 100. There's no in-between. Nobody scores a C+ or a B-. It's an A+ or you fail the whole course. Anybody who tells you differently hasn't confronted the true standard of the Law:

> *Again I declare to every man who lets himself be circumcised that he is **obligated** to obey the **whole** law.* (Galatians 5:3)

Voluntarily receiving the Jewish rite of circumcision meant you were placing yourself under the Law. Here, Paul wants us to know that's a commitment to keep the whole Law, not just part of it. Cherry-picking from the Law or treating it like the buffet line at your favorite restaurant isn't an option. If you're under the Law, you're obligated to keep the *whole* thing:

> For all who rely on the works of the law are **under a curse**, as it is written: "Cursed is everyone who does not continue to do **everything written in the Book of the Law**." (Galatians 3:10)

Paul describes being under the Law as being under a *curse*. Why? He says you're cursed if you don't do everything written in "the Book of the Law." This expression "Book of the Law" refers to the first five books of the Old Testament and every regulation contained within them.

In total, there are 613 commands and regulations in the Book of the Law. Paul is saying nobody has the right to pick out their favorite parts of the Law (the Ten Commandments, the Sabbath, tithing) while ignoring the rest of the Law. No, the Law invites you to experience all its demands at once. The reason? To show you that its standard is both perfect and impossible.

Anyone who flirts with a few choice laws from the Old Testament is just kidding themselves. That was never the invitation. The Law is an all-or-nothing proposition. That's precisely why no one survives being under it!

Breeding Ground

There's even more brilliance to God's giving the Law. He not only gave it as a perfect and impossible standard; He gave it to lovingly reveal our addiction to sin apart from Him. Expect more sinning under the Law, not less.

> *The law was brought in so that the trespass might increase. But where sin increased, grace increased all the more.* (Romans 5:20)

If you place yourself under the Law, you can expect sin to increase, not decrease. Why? Because the Law demands that human effort spring into action, and the inevitable result is failure. Put yourself under the Law, and you'll fail every single time. That's because being under the Law *arouses* sinful passions.

> *For when we were in the realm of the flesh, **the sinful passions aroused by the law** were at work in us, so that we bore fruit for death.* (Romans 7:5)

You read that one right: Sinful passions are *aroused* by the Law. When you're invited to a life of Law, you're invited to a life of sin. Paul expresses it this way:

> *But sin, **seizing the opportunity afforded by the commandment**, produced in me every kind of coveting. For apart from the law, sin was dead.* (Romans 7:8)

Did you catch that? Sin seizes an opportunity through the commandment. The Law affords sin an opportunity to thrive. No, the Law itself is not sin. But you put yourself under the Law, and sin will have a heyday as it masters you every time!

> *For sin shall no longer be your master,* **because you are not under the law,** *but under grace.* (Romans 6:14)

Do you see the reason sin masters you? It's when you choose to live under the Law. When won't sin master you? When you choose to live under God's grace. Have you considered the possibility that your struggle with sin relates to the way you're fighting it? If you fight sin with laws and rules, it always leads to failure.

> *The sting of death is sin, and* **the power of sin is the law.** (1 Corinthians 15:56)

The power of sin is enhanced under the Law. Sin is excited under the Law. The Law breeds defeat if you're honest and hypocrisy if you're not. It's only *apart* from the Law that sin is truly dead (Romans 7:8).

Freedom!

In Galatians, Paul describes the fruit of the Spirit and then says, "Against such things there is no law" (Galatians 5:23). If we're trusting God's Spirit and bearing fruit, we're going to be expressing love to people. We can't love them and steal from them. We can't love them and cheat on them. Love covers a multitude of sins (1 Peter 4:8).

We're called to this simple, powerful freedom. God wants us to enjoy it to the fullest and not settle in the least:

> *It is for **freedom** that Christ has set us free. **Stand firm**, then, and **do not let yourselves** be burdened again by a yoke of slavery.* (Galatians 5:1)

CHAPTER 7

I was leading an adult Bible class on 2 Corinthians. The first few weeks had gone well, but now we'd arrived at the chapter where Paul first talks about the Law. One of the people in the class, a man named James, was having some problems with it.

"I know the Bible says we're not under the Law, but you're talking about the Ten Commandments here. Are you saying we just disregard them?" James asked. "That we can just go out and murder and lie and steal?"

His face was incredulous; he was shocked. And no wonder: We lived in a small town where many people felt strongly that the Ten Commandments should be posted in public buildings and schools to show people what godly behavior looked like. Yet here we were, in Sunday Bible class, reading an epistle from the Apostle Paul himself, who said these laws … killed? *The Ten Commandments kill?!* This was too much for him to wrap his head around.

"We should still follow the Ten Commandments and ask for God's help to keep them," James argued. "They are the very backbone of Christianity!" You could tell he was convinced that yanking the Ten Commandments away from a believer would undoubtedly lead to lying and stealing and maybe even murder. Yet there it was, in black and white on the page before us: "the ministry that brought death" (2 Corinthians 3:7).

So who's right? Are the Ten Commandments an exception to our freedom from the Law? Is there nothing else to stabilize the believer's conduct besides tablets of stone?

The Ten Commandments

It's not just the 603 "other" regulations of the Law that kill. The Ten Commandments are a ministry of condemnation and death. In 2 Corinthians 3, Paul specifically refers to the ministry "engraved in letters on stone." Now, remember that the Ten Commandments were the only part of the Law written on stone:

> Now if **the ministry that brought death**, which was **engraved in letters on stone**, came with glory, so that the Israelites could not look steadily at the face of Moses because of its glory, transitory though it was, will not the ministry of the Spirit be even more glorious? If **the ministry that brought condemnation** was glorious, how much more glorious is the ministry that brings righteousness! For what was glorious has **no glory now**

in comparison with the surpassing glory. And if what was transitory came with glory, how much greater is the glory of that which lasts! (2 Corinthians 3:7–11)

Paul calls this ministry on stone "the ministry that brought death" and "the ministry that brought condemnation." That's pretty clear: The Ten Commandments bring condemnation and death.

Is that what you want in your life? Of course not! Especially when you're told the New Covenant ministry of God's Spirit brings righteousness and is more glorious than the Ten Commandments. You're only qualified to enjoy and minister one message: the New Covenant. Why would you want anything else?

*He has made us competent as **ministers of a new covenant**—not of the letter but of the Spirit; for **the letter kills**, but the Spirit gives life.* (2 Corinthians 3:6)

"The letter" refers to the Law, specifically the Ten Commandments. Those things kill, but the Spirit gives life. We're meant to celebrate and minister life to people, not death. We're ministers of a new covenant. Plus, consider this plain reality: Most who claim we're still under "the moral law" can't even recite the Ten Commandments, much less keep them!

The Truth about the Ten

So what should your spiritual relationship with the Ten Commandments be like? Non-existent! As a believer, you should make a clean break from Law-based living, and the Ten Commandments are *no exception*.

How can we be so sure? Well, in addition to what we already saw about the Ten Commandments as a ministry of condemnation and death, we find even more evidence in Romans 7:

> *What shall we say, then? Is the law sinful? Certainly not! Nevertheless, I would not have known what sin was had it not been for the law. For I would not have known what* **coveting** *really was if the law had not said,* **"You shall not covet."** *But* **sin, seizing the opportunity afforded by the commandment,** *produced in me every kind of coveting.* **For apart from the law, sin was dead.** (Romans 7:7–8)

Here, Paul is clearly talking about one of the Ten Commandments—the "You shall not covet" command. He says three important things here:

1. The Law showed him what sin was.
2. Sin seizes an opportunity through the Law.
3. Apart from the Law, sin is dead.

Now, given that Paul focuses on "You shall not covet" as his prime example, we can easily conclude the following in context:

1. The Ten Commandments showed him what sin was.

2. Sin seizes an opportunity through the Ten Commandments.

3. Apart from the Ten Commandments, sin is dead.

These should not be controversial statements today. It is plain and obvious from both 2 Corinthians 3 and Romans 7 that we're not to live under the Ten Commandments. And if we choose to do so, we experience "the ministry that brought death" and "the ministry that brought condemnation" as sin seizes an opportunity within us. It's only apart from the Ten Commandments that we can live free from sin.

The Bottom Line

Doesn't this make you wonder why there are so many believers who think the Ten Commandments help them fight sin? Here's the true effect of the Ten Commandments in a person's life:

> Once I was alive apart from the law; but **when the commandment came, sin sprang to life and I died**. I found that the very commandment that was intended to bring life actually **brought death**. For **sin, seizing the opportunity afforded by the commandment**, deceived me, and through the commandment **put me to death**. (Romans 7:9–11)

Keep in mind we're in Romans 7, and "You shall not covet" is the context. Paul is saying he felt like he was doing just fine until the commandment came into his life (first, as a young

Pharisee) and brought him death. The commandment gave sin an opportunity to spring to life and put him to death.

Now, the Law is not sin (Romans 7:7), but sin thrives under the Law (Romans 7:8, 11). If I invite you to a life of Law, I invite you to a life of sin. The Law kills, and the Ten Commandments are no exception.

CHAPTER 8

You don't often see an entire congregation with their mouths hanging open, but it happened that Sunday. I was speaking at a large church in the Northeast, and someone didn't like what I had to say—so right in the middle of the sermon, he jumped up and let me have it.

"You don't know what you're talking about!" he yelled. I stopped, and he continued in a slightly lower tone. "The Law reveals God's character. Yes, we're freed from the ceremonial law, but we're still under the moral law. What you're teaching is wrong. It's *antinomianism*," he concluded—an epithet I've heard a few times before.

I'm not sure the congregation had ever seen someone stand up and shout like that, so it made quite an impression. But it was an opportunity too: Everyone wanted to know how I'd reply. I gathered myself to address his concern, but even as the first words were coming out of my mouth, he bolted out of the auditorium. (After the service, to his credit, he met me in the hallway to apologize. "I'm sorry, brother," he said. "I really don't know what got into me!")

Is this grace message some sort of Law-bashing or Law-hating? Is it what's known as "antinomianism" (anti-Law-ism)? No, in fact, it's the opposite. What you see communicated here is Law-respecting, not Law-bashing. Think about it: Which person truly respects the Law?

A) The person who selects nine commandments (deleting the Sabbath), ten commandments, or eleven commandments (the Ten plus tithing) out of all the 613 commands and acts as if this is enough.

or

B) The person who confronts all 613 commands as a perfect and therefore impossible standard and decides they need God's grace instead.

Which person truly respects the Law? It's only those who see the Law as God does—as an all or nothing proposition—who truly respect it. Everyone else is kidding themselves.

The Law is holy and righteous and good (Romans 7:12). As Paul says, by choosing faith we do hold up the Law on a pedestal (Romans 3:31). We recognize its perfect and impossible standard. In this way, we hold the Law in high regard. The person who truly respects the Law is the one who opts for grace instead. After all, the Law is not made for believers; it's made to show unbelievers their sinfulness and need for grace:

> *We know that the law is good if one uses it properly. We also know that **the law is made not for the righteous***

but for lawbreakers and rebels, the ungodly and sin-
ful.... (1 Timothy 1:8–9a)

Not a Jot. Not a Tittle.

I was on a break—literally—during a conference. I was in the restroom, but the man at the urinal beside me wasn't ready for the conference session to end!

"Jesus said neither a jot nor a tittle of the Law would go away until Heaven and Earth disappear, so the Law is not done away with like you claim," he said with conviction and a satisfied air. "You're wrong, and the words of Jesus Himself prove it!"

He didn't say "gotcha!" but it hovered in the air, as if he'd caught me pulling a fast one and wasn't going to let me get away with it.

"Well, maybe we can talk about it further when we're not in the men's room," I said with a smile but also making my point. But this man could *not* wait. When I stepped out of the restroom, there he was, waiting to continue.

"You're right about what Jesus said," I agreed. "Neither a jot nor a tittle of the Law will disappear until Heaven and Earth disappear. And last time I checked, Heaven and Earth are still here, and so is the Law. So, I agree with you there. The Law is not dead."

This took him by surprise. He hadn't expected me to agree—but why wouldn't I? It's what the Bible says, after all.

I didn't stop there, though. I continued, "Here's the part you're missing: We Christians have died *to* the Law. That's a big difference."

He looked at me, puzzled. "So you're not saying the Law is done away with?"

"Of course not," I said. "We both know what the Bible says. But you're only looking at half of the picture."

The Law is not dead or gone. It's still here today. The Law is a tool to help unbelievers realize their need for Christ. The Law is not dead; it's *we believers* who have died *to the Law*. Plus, Jesus fulfilled the Law for us, I explained, so we don't need to fulfill it. He already did!

The man nodded as he contemplated the distinction, stepped aside, and motioned for me to proceed to the next session of the conference.

The Law Is Not for You!

At salvation, our death with Jesus separated us forever from Law-based living. We died to the Law so that we might live to God (Romans 7:4).

As I shared with that gentleman, the Law is very much alive and well today. Romans 7:12 says the Law is holy and righteous and good. It's just that the Law is for *unbelievers*, not Christians (1 Timothy 1:7–9). Galatians explains it this way:

> *Before the coming of this faith*, *we were held in custody under the law, locked up **until the faith** that was to come would be revealed. So, the law was our guardian **until Christ came** that we might be justified by faith. **Now that this faith has come**, we are no longer under a guardian.* (Galatians 3:23–25)

Even as Gentiles who had no formal law from God, the righteous requirements of the Law were written on our conscience, and they accused us as we sought to defend ourselves (Romans 2:15). But in Christ we have died to the Law (Galatians 2:19). Therefore, we have been freed from the Law. Now we serve in the new way of God's Spirit (Romans 7:4, 6).

> But if you are **led by the Spirit**, you are **not under the law**. (Galatians 5:18)

Early in Romans 7, Paul explains that the Law has no jurisdiction over a corpse (verses 1 and 4). A police officer won't likely write a speeding ticket for a dead man. Why not? Because he has died to the law, and he's no longer under its jurisdiction. Likewise, we were made to die to the Law so it would have no jurisdiction over us (Romans 7:4).

The Bottom Line

The Law is not dead, but we believers died *to the Law*. We're not under the Law. Christ is the end of the Law for us. None of the Law has been done away with, but it is exclusively for the *unbeliever* (1 Timothy 1:8–11). We believers are under grace and led daily by God's Spirit.

CHAPTER 9

I host a call-in show every weeknight. It's broadcast on SiriusXM and on radio stations around North America. We also stream it on Facebook and YouTube and in our mobile app so people can listen from all over the world.

As you can imagine, I get all kinds of interesting calls. They range from people wondering about relatively trivial issues like whether they should take their baby out of the service if he or she is crying (the answer to that is *yes*) to extremely critical questions like whether they've lost their salvation if they got divorced (the answer to that is *no*).

One night, Sandy from Toronto called in to our nightly broadcast with this question: "As a former Catholic, I really was never raised with the Old Testament. My husband and I are saved, and we spend a lot of time in the New Testament seeking to understand Paul's letters. But sometimes we may read a Psalm before we go to bed at night. Is the Old Testament for Jews? Or is it part of the overall Gospel message?"

That's a great question. Because we're not under the Law, is the Old Testament now irrelevant to us? Should it be ignored, even discarded? And if not, then where's the value in it?

The Old Testament

Here's the gist of what I shared with Sandy:

> *All Scripture is God-breathed and is useful for teaching, rebuking, correcting, and training in righteousness, so that the servant of God may be thoroughly equipped for every good work.* (2 Timothy 3:16–17)

All Scripture from Genesis to Revelation is God-breathed and inspired by the Holy Spirit. When Paul penned these words, he was clearly including the Old Testament, because it was all they had.

There's so much value in studying the Old Testament:

- It tells us how we as the human race got here: we were handcrafted by God, who spoke us into existence.
- We learn of Adam and Eve's rebellion against God and all the chaos that ensued.
- We see God's heart of mercy as He pursued a relationship with Israel.

- In Psalms, we see a man after God's own heart,
  David, crying out to God and trusting Him.
- In Proverbs, we discover the wisdom of God and
  why it's so much better than human wisdom.

I could go on and on about the value of the Old Testament. Without a doubt, it's essential. It forms the backdrop for the New Testament as the birth, death, and resurrection of Jesus were prophesied about long ago. So yes, the entire Bible from beginning to end is inspired by God.

But here's the question: When you read the Old Testament, do you have your grace glasses on? If you don't, it won't make sense. We read Leviticus and its prohibitions concerning food, even as we enjoy a pork sandwich or shrimp cocktail. Why can we read Leviticus without following its instructions? Because we're aware of the surprise ending in the Bible that occurs through the cross and the resurrection. We live under the New Covenant, and we read the Old in light of the New.

This doesn't mean we disregard three-fourths of our Bible. It simply means we recognize the difference between the Old Covenant and the New Covenant. We realize what covenant we're under. This gives us context.

In Psalm 51, David begs the Lord not to take His Spirit away (Psalm 51:11). Yet under the New Covenant, Paul and Peter and James and John never worry about this. Why not? Because the Holy Spirit doesn't come and go like that under the New Covenant.

This is just one example of the benefit of being under the New. We have something better that Old Testament believers did not experience (Hebrews 11:37–40). This New Covenant is a better covenant founded on better promises (Hebrews 8:6).

Let's study and respect all of the Bible, from Genesis to Revelation. At the same time, when we read the 613 commands directed at Israel, let's recognize we're reading someone else's mail. Those were regulations given to a nation long ago, and we're not under them. Christ is the end of the Law for us (Romans 10:4), and we live under God's grace (Romans 6:14).

The Truth about Gentiles

Most people who are debating Law and grace are Gentiles (non-Jews) who were never given the Law to begin with! That's right: Gentiles were never invited to the Law. The Law was given to Israel. Ephesians 2:12 says we Gentiles were excluded from the commonwealth of Israel and strangers to the Old Covenant. And Romans states plainly that Gentiles had no Law (Romans 2:14).

Yet today, so many people who live thousands of miles from Israel, on this side of the Atlantic Ocean, are pushing for certain laws from the Old Testament? It's the wrong covenant, and it's the wrong audience. The Law was never given to the Gentile, but today both Jew and Gentile are invited to Jesus and His grace.

The Shadow and the Reality

When I stand out in our front yard, I can see my shadow on the ground. But the shadow is not me, and I'm not the shadow. It's nothing more than a two-dimensional representation of my outline. It gives you some clue as to what I look like, but it's not the real thing.

In the same way, the Law was just a shadow, and the reality is Christ:

> **The law is only a shadow** *of the good things that are coming—not the realities themselves. For this reason, it can never, by the same sacrifices repeated endlessly year after year, make perfect those who draw near to worship.* (Hebrews 10:1)

> *Therefore, do not let anyone judge you by what you eat or drink, or with regard to a religious festival, a New Moon celebration or a Sabbath day.* **These are a shadow of the things that were to come; the reality, however, is found in Christ**. (Colossians 2:16–17)

Why look to the shadow (the Law) when you have the reality (Christ)? Hebrews 8:6 says the New Covenant is superior. So why would we go for something inferior? If the New Covenant is better, why entertain something that's worse?

Jesus went to great lengths to die for our sins, to be raised from the dead, and to be seated at the right hand of God on our behalf. Isn't it time we respect His finished work and all it accomplished?

CHAPTER 10

When I was a teenager, my family had an exchange student from Spain live with us, and I went to Spain and lived there for a while too. I speak Spanish, eventually got a doctorate in Applied Linguistics, and taught Spanish for many years as a professor at various universities in the U.S.

That's how I found myself speaking at a Christian conference for leaders in Chihuahua, Mexico. There were only about forty pastors and missionaries in attendance on the first day, but by the second day the audience had grown to over two hundred people. There was excitement in the air as many were finding freedom in God's grace.

While we were on a break, I sipped my coffee at the front of the auditorium. When I looked up, I was surrounded by several leaders with scowls on their faces. It took just a few of their comments for me to realize what angered them the most: my insistence that believers are even free from the Ten Commandments.

"Espera un momento … hold on just a minute," one of them shouted at me. "You're taking things to an extreme. I agree the Holy Spirit doesn't want us to live under the whole book of Leviticus, but we should still follow the Ten Commandments, and we should ask for the Spirit's help to do so!"

"But Sabbath observance is included in the Ten Commandments, and you don't adhere to the Friday night through Saturday night Sabbath, do you?" I asked.

"Well, no," one of them replied.

"So then, it's the Nine Commandments you're under, deleting the Sabbath?" I asked.

My question lingered in the air for them to ponder as the host announced our return to the next session.

A Sabbath Day: One of the Ten

Most people who fight for the Ten Commandments to be the one holdout from the Law aren't really keeping the Ten anyway. For one thing, they're not remembering the Sabbath day and keeping it holy. Here's how Sabbath-keeping was supposed to look:

> *Remember the Sabbath day by keeping it holy. Six days you shall labor and do all your work, but the seventh day is a sabbath to the Lord your God. On it **you shall not do any work**, neither you, nor your son or daughter, nor your male or female servant, nor your animals, nor any foreigner residing in your towns.* (Exodus 20:8–10)

No Friday night emails. No Saturday yard work. No work done by you or your family members (or your animals!) for twenty-four hours. God instituted the Sabbath for Israel as part of the Law to remind them how God rested after the creation of the world:

> By the seventh day God had finished the work he had been doing; so, on the seventh day *He rested* from all his work. (Genesis 2:2)

Today's Spiritual Sabbath

Today, we're living under the New Covenant. We're called to a spiritual Sabbath, not a physical one.

> There remains, then, **a Sabbath-rest for the people of God**; for anyone who enters God's rest also **rests from their works**, just as God did from his. Let us, therefore, **make every effort to enter that rest**, so that no one will perish by following their example of disobedience. (Hebrews 4:9–11)

This is a spiritual rest. The author of Hebrews says we have had "good news proclaimed to us" (Hebrews 4:2) and that's why we should rest. What is the good news that brings rest? Total forgiveness brings rest. Living under God's grace brings rest. A God who will never leave us brings rest. It is the Gospel itself that brings rest. Jesus Himself invites us to rest:

> Come to me, all you who are weary and burdened, and **I will give you rest**. Take my yoke upon you and learn

*from me, for I am gentle and humble in heart, and you will find **rest** for your souls.* (Matthew 11:28–29)

The author of Hebrews warns the Jews of his day to not be like their forefathers, who wandered in the desert for forty years. They refused to believe God and enter the Promised Land. They refused to rest. The Hebrew author urges his readers not to be like their ancestors and instead "make every effort to enter that rest" (Hebrews 4:11).

This means decisions need to be made: *Do you believe Jesus has the authority and power to save you? How much confidence will you place in His cross? How forgiven do you believe you really are? How much confidence will you place in His resurrection? How secure is this new life you possess?*

These are questions the Hebrews needed to confront. These are questions each one of us needs to confront today. Our answers determine whether or not we spiritually relax in Jesus.

The Bottom Line

We're not under any obligation to keep a physical Sabbath. In fact, the Sabbath was given to Israel as a picture or shadow of the spiritual rest we can now enjoy:

*Therefore do not let anyone judge you by what you eat or drink, or with regard to a religious festival, a New Moon celebration or **a Sabbath day**. **These are a shadow of the things that were to come; the reality, however, is found in Christ**.* (Colossians 2:16–17)

Don't let anyone judge you or try to impose a Sabbath day on you. You are dead to the Law and therefore dead to the Old Covenant concept of Sabbath. You are not under the Law and therefore not under the Sabbath.

The Sabbath was required of the Jews under the Law. It was a symbol of a greater spiritual rest you now experience in Jesus. God saw His work in creation was good, and He rested. You too can see the finished work of Jesus Christ is good and rest from the frantic religious activity of trying to get right and stay right with God. You rest by agreeing with Jesus that "it is finished."

CHAPTER 11

Many emails I receive begin with a zinger, and this one was no exception.

"You are depriving God's children of their birthright!" Ron's email began. "Tithing is what opens up the windows of Heaven so God can pour out abundant blessings on His people. It is ignorant of you to teach others to neglect the tithe.

"The tithe and first fruits belong to God," Ron continued. "They unlock the spiritual realm where God rebukes Satan and keeps your finances protected. I have tested this and watched as God has proven Himself again and again, keeping my family from harm."

Ron's email went on to urge me to reconsider my teaching on grace-giving. Yes, another big holdout today—in addition to the Ten Commandments—is tithing.

To "tithe" (meaning "a tenth") is to give one-tenth of your income to God. Is this required? Is this mandated in the New Testament under God's grace? The short answer is *no*.

Maybe you've heard tithing is just the "starting place" under grace and we should give even more than 10 percent? While that sounds really spiritual, it's just not the truth. The Law is not the starting place for grace.

The Law does not set the benchmark for the New Covenant. If that were true, we would start with avoiding pork and shellfish and then graduate to avoiding other foods. If that were true, we would start with observing a Saturday Sabbath and then graduate to working less and less throughout the week.

Ridiculous! Tithing is not the starting place because grace is not stricter than the Law. *We really are free to live and give from the heart, and there is no minimum benchmark to hit.*

God owns the cattle on a thousand hills. He is over everything (Psalm 50:10). He's not served by human hands as if He needs anything (Acts 17:25). God is not up in Heaven wringing His hands, wondering when we're going to pay up. Colossians 2:14 says He canceled the debt that stood opposed to us. We don't owe God.

Robbing God?

But maybe you've seen somebody haul out this passage and tell you that you do owe God:

> *"Will a mere mortal rob God? Yet you rob me.*
> *"But you ask, 'How are we robbing you?'*

"In tithes and offerings. You are under a curse—your whole nation—because you are robbing me.

"Bring the whole tithe into the storehouse, that there may be food in my house. Test me in this," says the Lord Almighty, "and see if I will not throw open the floodgates of heaven and pour out so much blessing that there will not be room enough to store it." (Malachi 3:8–10)

In verse 8, God says to Israel, "You rob Me." Then verse 10 speaks of a huge blessing from bringing the tithe into the "storehouse." What does a storehouse hold? Grain. And that's precisely what an Old Testament tithe was about—food. Under the Law, God mandated that the other tribes of Israel donate food to support the tribe of Levitical priests. In turn, the Levites were not allowed to own their own property or take on extra jobs to earn additional income. Yet today there are some ministers preaching a required tithe while they own property and earn extra income—a total contradiction!

Interestingly, Malachi 3:9 is often left out of the picture. It says, "You are under a curse—your whole nation—because you are robbing me." We don't often hear the "curse" part of this passage. It's simply not mentioned, and neither is the "whole nation" part. But it's obvious God is addressing the nation of Israel, whereas you who are in Christ today don't need to worry about being under a curse. Christ redeemed you from the curse of the Law (Galatians 3:13), and you are blessed with every spiritual blessing (Ephesians 1:3).

God is not up in Heaven demanding a certain percentage of your income. God is not a divine slot machine. You don't pour in the tithe, pull down the handle, and wait for the blessings. You're not buying Him off like a mafioso who will protect your neighborhood or keep your family from harm if you pay enough. That's not a healthy perception of God for anyone to have!

What if the amount and frequency of your giving was decided by you, in your heart, in an atmosphere of freedom? That's grace-giving. As we'll see, that's been God's intention for His children all along.

The Truth about Tithing

There's no mention of a 10 percent requirement in any New Testament letter. And what we see in the four gospels is Jesus chastising the Jews for their hypocrisy in tithing their spices but neglecting the other parts of the Law. In so doing, Jesus says tithing is a matter of the Law (Matthew 23:23). He compares lighter matters of the Law (like tithing) with "weightier" matters of the Law. Definitively, tithing is a matter of the Law, but you as a believer are not under the Law. So you're not under the tithe, plain and simple.

Under the Law, giving ultimately totaled more than 21 percent. And it was more about giving food than money. So today when you see people pushing a 10 percent tithe of income, here's what you need to remember: (1) It's the wrong covenant, (2) it's the wrong percentage, and (3) it's the wrong currency.

Grace-Giving

Of course, you shouldn't spend your life sitting on your hands being stingy in the name of grace. So what motivates your giving? You get to be inspired at a heart level to give what you truly want to give.

Paul says the motivation for giving today under God's grace is an "eager willingness" and that you should only give "according to your means" and "according to what one has."

> *Now finish the work, so that **your eager willingness** to do it may be matched by your completion of it, according to your means. **For if the willingness is there, the gift is acceptable according to what one has, not according to what one does not have.** Our desire is **not** that others might be relieved while you are hard pressed, but that there might be equality.* (2 Corinthians 8:11–13)

God doesn't use manipulation. And He doesn't say, as many suggest, to "give until it hurts." In fact, Paul stressed that he didn't want anyone to be "hard pressed" in their giving (verse 13). He said they were free to give out of their "plenty" or excess (verse 14). That's radically different from the pressure tactics we often see today. So here's the truth: Give until it hurts? No, give out of your excess.

> *Each of you should give **what you have decided in your heart to give**, not reluctantly or under compulsion, for God loves a **cheerful** giver.* (2 Corinthians 9:7)

You're called to enjoy freedom in your giving. It should be about proclaiming the message and supporting the messengers (1 Corinthians 9:14). As far as tithing's being God's way of "testing your heart," here's the truth: God already knows your heart. He gave it to you! He knows it's a new, obedient, resurrection heart. He instructs you to simply "give what you have decided in your heart to give" (2 Corinthians 9:7).

This requires trust. You need to trust that God is moving in believers' hearts to inspire you (and others) to give. People often ask how our church survives without teaching a required tithe. We've taught grace-giving for two decades at our church, yet we make budget every year. I'd say we make it *because* we teach grace-giving, not despite it.

We make our needs known. We don't overspend. We don't plan wildly beyond our means and later resort to pressure. We simply let God inspire, and He does.

When people's lives are transformed, they want to see the same happen for others, so they give to the cause. This is how God designed grace-giving to happen within His church. Grace-giving is the same as grace-living. The motivation doesn't change when we get out our wallets!

CHAPTER 12

The man approached me with a determined look in his eye as I was signing books. "I appreciate your desire to communicate God's grace, *but . . .*" he began. With the "b" word I'd heard so many times, I immediately knew where this was going.

"But in the process, you're mixing up justification and sanctification," he continued. "Of course, we're not saved by the Law, but the Law still serves a purpose in pointing out sin to us and revealing where God's taking us in terms of growth."

I'd heard this before, so I cut right to the chase. "So, God is pointing out to you that eating pork and shellfish is sin? And God is leading you toward abstaining from those foods so you can grow in Him?"

"No, that's the dietary law," he retorted. "I'm talking about the *moral* law—the Ten Commandments."

I pressed further. "So, one of the Ten Commandments is the Sabbath. Is God pointing out to you that Saturday yard work is sin? Is He teaching you to abstain from Friday night emails and lawn mowing so you can grow in Him?"

"No, that's the Sabbath. Jesus fulfilled the Sabbath," he answered.

Even though things were already feeling a bit testy, I continued, "Okay, so let me get this straight: You believe somewhere in the New Testament it teaches believers to look to the *Nine* Commandments as our moral compass while not worrying about the other 604 commands in the Law?"

"Well, basically, yes. Otherwise, how would we know not to steal or murder?" he replied adamantly.

"So, you would otherwise want to steal from people and murder them, but it's tablets of stone from thousands of years ago that are stopping you?" I asked, just trying to get him to think.

"No, I don't want to murder anyone!" he exclaimed. "That's not the point!"

"Well, I think it is the point," I insisted. "It sounds like—with or without Moses—you don't want to steal or murder or cheat or anything else. You already have a 'moral compass' within you, and His name is Jesus."

I went on to explain how we believers don't have to go fishing through the Book of Leviticus to figure out whether to steal or to kill people. There are plenty of New Testament instructions that tell us exactly what to expect from God's Spirit who lives in us: things like love and patience and self-control. If we're bearing the fruit of the Spirit, we're not going to be stealing and killing people. The indwelling Christ is our moral compass.

He thought for a minute and asked, "So, you're not just saying we wake up and do whatever feels right in our own eyes—abuse or cheat on our spouse, for example—because there's an understanding of the character of Jesus and what He's like in us?"

"Exactly," I said. "It's not like we are wandering in the dark here. There are dozens of New Testament attitude and action passages about where Christ is leading us. We know exactly what the Spirit of God within us is moving us toward: namely, love. And love covers a multitude of sins. I can't love you and steal from you at the same time. I can't love you and abuse you at the same time. So, it's hardly a nebulous, chaotic, or uncontrolled life we're talking about here. We look to God's Spirit, depend on Him, and He always produces self-control within us."

A Simple Message

The Bible does speak clearly to the believer's "relationship" with the Law. The message is plain, and we shouldn't abandon its simplicity (2 Corinthians 11:3).

Here's your relationship to the Law:

- You're dead to the Law (Romans 7:4, 6; Galatians 2:19).
- You're not under the Law (Romans 6:14; Galatians 5:18).
- You're free from the Law (Romans 7:2, 4).

- You're not supervised by Law (Galatians 3:25).
- The requirements of the Law have been fully met in you (Romans 8:3–4).
- The Law is set aside (Ephesians 2:14–15; Hebrews 7:18).
- Christ is the end of the Law for you who believe (Romans 10:4).
- You don't serve in the old way of the Law (Romans 7:6).
- You serve in the newness and freedom of the Spirit (Romans 7:6; Galatians 5:13).

Even though we believers realize obedience to the Law doesn't save us, many of us still try to hold on to the Law for something else: as a moral compass, to define sin, or to help us grow in Christ.

What role should the Law play in our lives as believers? None. It cannot serve as our moral compass to define sin for us. The Law would define sin in 613 ways. Eating pork and shellfish would be sin, and working on Saturday would be sin. If we were to adopt the Law's definition of sin, we'd spend most of our day sinning. People don't even imagine what they're saying when they claim the Law defines sin for the believer. Plus, they consequently have to take on the role of God in choosing which Old Testament laws do and don't apply as the moral compass.

The Law certainly doesn't grow you up either. Galatians 3:3 asks: "Having begun by the Spirit, are you now being perfected by human effort?" The implication is that your human effort and Law-keeping is no way to grow in Christ. The Law is not your source, and the Law is not your goal. Knowing Christ is your source, and knowing and expressing Christ is your goal. It's about the fruit of the Spirit, not the works of the Law.

After salvation, you should have absolutely zero relationship with the Law. Still, what we see today are many believers looking to an almost arbitrary list of commands. For some, maybe it's the Ten Commandments. For others, they delete the Sabbath, and it's the Nine Commandments. Still others remove the Sabbath but add tithing—"Look, Ma, it's a new set of Ten!"

But here's the truth: We're dead to the Law. We're not under the Law. Christ is the end of the Law for us. This is not true just for salvation. It's true for daily living.

It's true, period.

The Bottom Line

Your death to the Law was the only way you could bear fruit for God (Romans 7:4). The Spirit within you now brings about a life the Law never could.

And when it comes to defining sin under the New Covenant, Romans 14 tells us that whatever is not of faith in Christ is sin (Romans 14:23). It's about fixing our eyes on the Son and being an expression of Him. We don't need Moses to show us what sin was when we've got Jesus to show us what righteousness is!

> But if you are **led by the Spirit**, you are not under the law. (Galatians 5:18)

CHAPTER 13

People often try to pass off their objections to the grace message under the guise of scholarship. One man took this approach with me to argue over the role of the Law and the New Covenant in our lives.

"The New Covenant is both a culmination and continuation of the Old," he insisted. "This is the scholarly view of the Law. What you're proposing about the Old and the New Covenants is not biblical. A more informed view recognizes the continuation of the Old into the New."

This is just one comment among the hundreds like it I've heard during my ministry. I guess it's normal to assume that if a person has taken a radical stance on an issue, they simply haven't investigated enough. It's easy to think more learning is needed to arrive at the proper "balance."

But when you study the Bible on the issue of the Old and New Covenants, what you find is radical. The language is strong. It becomes clear that you are not to be mixing the Old Covenant with the New Covenant in any sense.

Obsolete. Set Aside. Weak. Useless.

When was the last time you stopped by a video rental store? How about the last time you made a call in a phone booth? It's unlikely you've been in either one of these lately because they're *obsolete*. They've been replaced with new and better ways of doing things. Today, we have streaming movies and cell phones, so there's just no demand for movie rental stores and phone booths.

Likewise, the arrival of the New Covenant rendered the Old Covenant *obsolete*.

> *By calling this covenant "new," he has made the first one* **obsolete**; *and what is* **obsolete** *and* **outdated** *will soon disappear.* (Hebrews 8:13)

> *The former regulation is* **set aside** *because it was* **weak** *and* **useless** *(for the law made nothing perfect), and* **a better hope** *is introduced, by which we draw near to God.* (Hebrews 7:18–19)

You have something "better" today, a better covenant founded on better promises:

> *But in fact the ministry Jesus has received is as* **superior** *to theirs as the covenant of which he is mediator is*

*superior to the old one, since the new covenant is estab-lished on **better promises***. (Hebrews 8:6)

The Law is obsolete, weak, and useless to make anyone perfect. So, it has been set aside (Hebrews 7:18–19). Why would you look to something inferior when you have some-thing superior? That would make no sense! You relate to God through something so much better in the New.

Is the Law on Your Heart?

Becky had already sat through about three hours of my teaching on law and grace at a Saturday seminar. But there was one thing she couldn't get over.

"I understand what you're saying about us being under grace now, but we do have God's Law written on our hearts," she declared, convinced of what she had been taught. "We can't keep the Law on our own, but as believ-ers we have God's Spirit living in us. He will help us obey His Law."

Despite what she'd heard from me so far, she was still entertaining the possibility that God had written the Law on her heart.

"Becky, do you have 'no mixed fabrics' and 'no crab cakes' written on your heart? Or how about 'no Saturday gardening' and 'no gardening at all with mingled seeds'? Are those writ-ten on your heart? Do you think God's Spirit is helping you keep the 613 commands of the Old Testament law? And if so, how's it going?" I asked, hoping to get right to the "heart" of the issue.

"I do see what you're saying," she relented, "That makes sense. But it does leave a question: The Bible says He writes His laws on our hearts, so what does that mean then?"

That's the perfect question to ask: What *is* written on your heart today?

What's in Your Heart?

Remember from Chapter Two: The New Covenant is a *download* and a *deletion*. God downloads His desires to your heart, and He deletes your sin record altogether. That's the New Covenant in a nutshell. That's what it means to be God's child—a new creation.

In Hebrews 10, we read that God's *laws* (plural, not the singular *Law*) are etched on the lining of our new spiritual hearts. But what "laws" are these?

The 613 commands of the Law are not written on your heart. No, it's something altogether different written within you. Jesus gives a new command in John 13:34, saying we're called to love others as He loves us. And John picks up this same idea:

> *And this is His command: **to believe** in the name of His Son, Jesus Christ, and **to love** one another as He commanded us.* (1 John 3:23)

To believe and to love: these are the laws written on our hearts. We're invited to get to know how much God loves us and soak in that love. Only then can we transmit that kind of love (God's love!) to other people.

These laws of "believe and love" are known as "the royal law" (James 2:8) or "His commands" (1 John 3:24), and they aren't burdensome (1 John 5:3). In fact, we find Jesus saying that those who love Him (believers) *will* obey His commands (John 14:15). It seems to happen (super)naturally and almost automatically. It's who we are.

It's not the no-pork or no-shellfish or no-work-on-Saturday law that is written on your heart. No, the new commands of *believe* and *love* inspire you today under the New Covenant. These commands on your heart are more than enough since love is the true fulfillment of the Law (Romans 13:10). Love covers a multitude of sins (1 Peter 4:8). You can't love someone and murder them. You can't love them and cheat on them. As we walk in the love of Christ, everything else takes care of itself.

Not Those Two Either!

By the way, people often think the two commands written on our hearts are *to love your God with all your heart and soul and strength* and *to love your neighbor as yourself* (Matthew 22).

Here's the truth: Those commands came up in a conversation between Jesus and the Pharisees. They asked Jesus which were the greatest commands *in the Law*, and He offered those as His reply. So let's not forget that those commands are *in the Law* (Matthew 22:37–40). Imagine waking up every day and *trying your hardest* to love God with all your being and to love others as much as you love yourself. Jesus was saying these are the two greatest (and most impossible!) commands in the Law.

You are not under the Law. You don't want Law-based living, whether it's the least or the greatest commands in the Law. What you enjoy are the New Covenant commands of "believe" and "love" written on your heart.

If you were curious about loving God with all your heart, God took care of that one for you. Ephesians 6:24 says that now as a new creation in Christ, you actually have *an undying love* for Jesus built into your heart. God caused you to love Him permanently. He poured out His love in your heart (Romans 5:5). You love Him because He first loved you and deposited His love in you forever (1 John 4:19).

The Bottom Line

It makes no sense to say you died to the Law and then turn right around and say the Law is written on your heart. You don't have something on your heart that you're dead to!

The Holy Spirit is *not* helping you keep the Law. It's simply not His agenda.

Instead, He is inspiring you to bear the fruit of the Spirit, and "against such things there is no law" (Galatians 5:23). God couldn't make it any clearer: "But if you are led by the Spirit, you are not under the law" (Galatians 5:18).

CHAPTER 14

A few years ago, I was speaking to a student ministry group at a university in Canada. When I was a student myself, I spent a lot of time figuring out what I believed. I was part of an InterVarsity Christian Fellowship group, and when I became a professor, I served as our local chapter's faculty advisor for many years, so I always welcomed the opportunity to speak with students.

After I'd finished, I was approached by Matthew, an engineering student who said he'd been attending the group for a few years. I'd seen him taking notes through the whole talk, but it was clear he still had some questions that needed answering.

"I do understand your teaching that we're not under the Law, but we still need the Law as our moral compass to stay on track," he insisted. "Without the Law as guardrails, how would we ever know how God was leading us?"

I could tell that Matthew was genuine in wanting to truly please God, and he didn't want to get it wrong.

"What if I told you the Spirit of God is always leading you toward expressing Him—love, patience, self-control, and all of the beautiful things that He is? So why would you even need the Law?" I asked.

"Yeah, but without a system of rules or principles to guide, it just seems uncertain." Matthew stopped and pondered. He was thinking this through, even though it contradicted the way he'd been approaching the issue for years.

"Well, maybe that's part of the beauty of it," I proposed.

I went on to explain to him that, as Christians, we are proving that the invisible God lives in us when—*without* the intervention of rules or principles to follow—we end up living in a godly way and loving others.

The Bible literally says "the Law is not based on faith" (Galatians 3:12). It takes no faith at all to keep a bunch of rules or laws. But when we by faith express the life of Jesus to others, we serve as evidence of God's presence in our lives. The invisible life of Christ shows up in visible ways in our attitudes and actions, offering evidence that He is risen and lives in us today.

"Christianity is not about rules. It's about letting Christ rule," I said. He rules in our hearts by faith (Colossians 3:15).

Matthew nodded and said I'd given him a lot to think about.

What about Rules?

You know what I hate? When telemarketers call my cell phone. There I am, in the middle of my day, and suddenly I'm interrupted by someone calling my cell phone illegally.

Yes, *illegally*. If you don't know already, placing telemarketing calls to a wireless phone is—and always has been—illegal in most cases.

In the United States, you can put your cell number on the Federal Communications Commission's national Do Not Call list, which will prevent at least some of the those deceptive sales pitches. Many scammers even use spoofing software to make it seem like they're calling from a local number so you'll answer.

Spiritually, many masquerade as messengers of God who are trying to "market" the idea that we need rules to keep us on the right road with God. We end up answering the call, becoming suckers for the sales pitch of lifeless religion. We start to think if we just adhere to a few rules (do your quiet time, go to church, give money) and avoid bad behavior, we're successfully navigating the Christian life.

The truth is that any laundry list of dos and don'ts yields the same result in our lives:

> *Since you died with Christ to the elemental spiritual forces of this world, why, as though you still belonged to the world, do you submit to its rules: "Do not handle! Do not taste! Do not touch!"? These rules, which have to do with things that are all destined to perish with use, are based on merely human commands and teachings. Such regulations indeed have **an appearance of wisdom**, with their self-imposed worship, their false humility and their harsh treatment of the body, **but they lack any value in restraining sensual indulgence**.* (Colossians 2:20–23)

Do not handle. Do not taste. Do not touch. Rules like these seem so spiritual but don't really help in restraining sin. How about an experiment to prove it? For the next fifteen seconds, here's one rule to obey: *Don't think about a purple leprechaun.*

No purple leprechauns, okay? Ready, go!

Now, even as you're reading this, you're struggling, right? Let's face it: When you opened this book today, you were leprechaun-free. You hadn't thought about a leprechaun one single time. Now, all of a sudden, it's Lucky Charms everywhere you turn!

The Truth about Rules

I shared that silly (but effective!) experiment to make the point. Now, here's an example from everyday life.

What's the first thing you think of when you see a road sign? You probably don't think to pull out a gun and shoot it. But a friend of mine once shared with me that, as he was jeeping on the mining trails of Colorado, he encountered a sign on the side of the road that read, "No Shooting Next 4 Miles." It was barely readable. Why? Because it had dozens of bullet holes in it!

There's no better way to inspire someone to do something than to tell them not to do it. Sin masters people who are under rule-based obedience. The Bible goes so far as to say that "the power of sin is the law" (1 Corinthians 15:56). Sin takes *opportunity* through the commandment (Romans 7:8, 11).

But if rules don't inspire godliness, what does? Remember, God has that covered:

*For sin shall **not** be master over you, for you are not under law but **under grace**.* (Romans 6:14)

When you have Jesus living within you, you're not under the Law. You're under grace. Apart from the Law, sin is dead. Under grace, righteousness thrives in you!

The Origin of Rules

Our modern-day, rule-based forms of Christianity are no better than living under the Jewish Law with its 613 commands. Either way, the Law kills.

Where did measuring and improving ourselves come from? It began a long time ago in a garden far, far away. In Genesis 3, we read that Satan seduced Adam and Eve. The first humans were suckers for the sales pitch of self-   improvement. Satan's pitch went like this: "For God knows that when you eat from [the tree] your eyes will be opened, and you will be like God, knowing good and evil" (Genesis 3:5).

Satan didn't sell them on doing something *bad*. No, it was all couched in the idea of being *good*, like God. They weren't choosing to eat from "the evil tree." They were eating from the tree of the knowledge of *good* and evil. Their goal was not to be like Satan. Their goal was to be like God. You might even say their goal was to be more "godly."

With that, they were sunk. They were already innocent and flawless and complete, but they chose to believe a lie. They thought God was holding out on them. They believed they could better their condition. So they ate from the tree, began measuring themselves by a standard they were never meant for, and inevitably felt shame. They went and hid in their nakedness. God arrived on the scene and asked, "Who told you that you were naked?" (Genesis 3:11).

If you're not careful, you can believe the same lie. When you fail to put confidence in your righteousness and completeness in Christ, you begin seeking to measure and "improve" yourself in a way God never intended. You look to rules and restrictions as a means of bettering yourself. But God doesn't want you eating from the tree of the knowledge of good and evil. There was another tree in that garden, and you might say you've already eaten of the "tree of life in Christ Jesus." So you're in no need of self-improvement.

The Bottom Line

You live under grace. You stand in grace. You enjoy grace upon grace. God's grace is more than sufficient for you (2 Corinthians 12:9). You can't get any more right than righteous. You can't get any more forgiven than "once for all." You can't get any newer than a new creation.

You can simply believe it and be satisfied with all God has done for you and in you to make you His own.

CHAPTER 15

"Under your theology, nothing happens to me if I do wrong. So, why not just go out and sin? There's nothing stopping me from living like the devil!" Linda exclaimed.

I had only been on national radio a little while, and a woman named Linda from Georgia was calling in to ask her question and put my teaching to the test.

"Live like the devil? You're not like the devil, are you, Linda?" I asked.

That stopped her in her tracks. I took advantage of the brief silence to continue.

Then I said, "But, seriously, Linda, I don't blame you for asking the question. In fact, any theology that doesn't beg this question is legalism. I mean, if we believe all the punishment for our sins fell on Jesus, and there's no condemnation left, it's logical to ask: Then why behave?"

"Yeah, so I've got my fire insurance now," she snapped. "What's stopping me from doing whatever I want?"

"I hear you," I replied. "So, now we have to have ask: What do you really want? Plus, has the fear of fire been the main thing restraining you from setting world records for sin?"

There was another moment of silence, and then Linda answered, "Well, no, not really."

"Linda, the Apostle Paul asked the same question you're asking," I said. "In Romans 6, he asked: 'Shall we go on sinning so that grace may increase?' Of course, Paul's answer is, 'By no means!' But what's most interesting are his reasons for not sinning. None of them are threats!"

"What do you mean?" Linda inquired.

"Well, Paul doesn't say you should not sin because God will be angry with you," I said, "and he doesn't say you'll lose your salvation. He doesn't say God will punish you or that you'll be 'out of fellowship' either. He doesn't give any of those reasons for not sinning."

"What's his reason then?" she asked.

"Okay, here's the reason Paul gives for choosing to live uprightly," I said. "'We died to sin. How can we live in it any longer? Or do you not know . . . ?' From there, Paul asks if they know what happened to them at salvation: They were *crucified* and *buried* and *raised* to newness of life."

"So, we're just supposed to believe we died to sin?" Linda asked, following the logic but still not convinced.

"Well, yes. You're going to prove God is right about you, one way or another: by sinning and being miserable or by displaying Jesus and being fulfilled."

Either way, I explained, you prove God is right about you. Plus, Paul's point in Romans 6 is that it's pure insanity to continue to choose sin when you're new-hearted and born of God. It makes no sense to act like you're a slave to sin when you're a slave of righteousness. Later, in the same chapter, Paul essentially asks: What benefit is there to sin anyway? The outcome is never good, so why would you want that?

You *don't* really want it. That's the truth!

Linda told me I'd given her a lot to think about. It takes time to absorb all this, but she was willing to reconsider. And I understood: This runs counter to so much we've heard over the years, and sometimes it takes a while to "unlearn" the old and accept the new.

Views of Sin

The immature view of sin is that the world is "living it up." They're having a great time, and you're stuck over here being a Christian. God is holding out on you.

But here's the reality: God has the market cornered on fulfillment. He wants the best for you. When God calls you to a new way of upright living, He's looking out for you. God knows who you are, and He wants you to experience His best. And when it comes to behavior, He's simply showing you *what to wear*—what is "fitting" for a saint:

> *Therefore, as God's chosen people, holy and dearly loved,* **clothe yourselves** *with compassion, kindness, humility, gentleness, and patience.* (Colossians 3:12)

*But fornication and all uncleanness or covetousness, let it not even be named among you, as is **fitting for saints**.* (Ephesians 5:3 NKJV)

Grieving or Quenching the Spirit

While God is not going to "getcha," there are obvious consequences to sin. First, you can't express sin and express Jesus at the same time. Impossible! So when you choose sin, you're not choosing Him in that moment.

In Ephesians 4, Paul says not to *grieve* the Holy Spirit. In context, he's saying to build others up with wholesome, encouraging words. He's saying not to allow bitterness to take root but to instead forgive others (Ephesians 4:29–32). Grieving the Spirit is when God's Spirit has deep concern for you and wants better for you in your relationships. His grieving over you is not anger toward you. You've been saved completely from the anger of God (Romans 5:9). The Spirit is grieved (deeply concerned) over you because sin is beneath you, and He knows it. You're better than sin, and God simply wants His best for you. So thank God that He's deeply concerned for you. Imagine if He weren't!

In 1 Thessalonians 5, Paul says not to *quench* the Spirit. In context, he's saying to hold on to what is good, celebrate Jesus, give thanks in everything, and always talk transparently with God in prayer (1 Thessalonians 5:16–22). To quench the Spirit is to hinder the expression of Christ. This happens when we don't set our minds on God's goodness and grace. Then we miss out on the thankfulness God longs for us to enjoy. Simply put, you can't express sin and Jesus at the same time.

The Bottom Line

You don't need a "God's gonna getcha" message to live uprightly. You don't need someone dangling the promise of heavenly jewelry or more square footage in your mansion to motivate you. You don't need to be bribed to avoid sin.

You simply need to know (and believe) who you really are and then just be yourself. You're dead to sin and alive to God, and that'll become obvious one way or another. So why not save yourself the time and frustration of sin? Why not go ahead and do what you *really* want?

People who question God's grace have a miniscule view of it. Sure, if we told the whole world, "You're forgiven," they would live like animals. But what if we did more than share a message of forgiveness? What if, by some miracle, we could reach into their very beings and transform who they are and what they desire? That's exactly what God's grace has done for us!

So, saying we should tone down God's grace is like saying we should tone down our new hearts or tone down our victory over sin. It just makes no sense!

PART 2

KILLER SERMON

CHAPTER 16

"I've been trying to follow Jesus my whole life," Ruth confessed. "I just can't do it anymore!"

She was sitting across from me in a café at the hotel where I'd just given a conference. The final session had just ended, and she'd asked if I had time to talk before I headed off to another speaking engagement that night.

"What do you mean, Ruth?" I replied. "You're a believer, and you're learning and growing just like the rest of us."

"Yes, but when I read what Jesus said about being sold out to Him, my life just doesn't compare," she said. "Selling everything, loving my enemies, praying for people who hate me, turning the other cheek? I just can't do it."

"Have you considered the possibility that *nobody* can do those things?" I asked.

Ruth looked puzzled. "What do you mean?"

"Well, Jesus was born under the Old Testament Law, and His audience was under Old Testament Law," I said. "Sometimes, when Jesus was talking to them, His goal was to show the Jews the *impossible* standard of God's Law that nobody could actually live up to.

"You're not alone in your struggle," I told her. "You're only alone in that most people today sweep that impossible standard under the rug and act like they're doing just fine. You've simply admitted you can't live up to it. Now you're ready to understand the difference between the old way and the new way of relating to God."

Ruth looked intrigued, so I continued explaining the difference. By the time we had finished talking, you could literally see the relief on her face. The truth had set her free.

What If . . . ?

Like Ruth, I was taught, as most of us are, that the teachings of Jesus are a palatable mixture of prophecies, parables, and loving rebukes. I understood them all as having the same context and intention—to instruct Jews long ago and Christians today in the ways of God.

Once I started to read and study the Bible for myself, I was surprised to see that Jesus's teachings don't always dovetail with the message of grace in the New Testament. Sometimes they flat-out contradict what the epistles say. Why?

The more I searched and studied, the more urgent the burning question became: Did Jesus intentionally, in His teachings, set a standard He knew no one could ever meet?

As the most prominent example, what if most of today's religious interpretations get the Sermon on the Mount wrong? What if Jesus never expected anyone, including the twenty-first-century Christian, to follow the radical commands of His mountainside treatise?

These are potentially life-transforming claims, and as such, they require serious and thoughtful investigation (which we'll conduct over the next few chapters). Some may get offended, mistakenly believing I'm suggesting we randomly disregard portions of the four gospels. Others may understand me yet vehemently disagree. Many, however, will discover a tremendous relief; because ultimately, no matter how we view the impossible teachings of Jesus, no one to this day is living up to them.

If we Christians were living out the impossible teachings of Jesus today, we would be easily identifiable due to our missing eyes and limbs. We would be giving money to whoever requests it of us. Church lawns would be home to countless yard sales as we disposed of all our worldly possessions.

Clearly, this isn't happening. So, what has the Church traditionally done with these impossible teachings of Jesus? Most interpret them as hyperbole or exaggeration. But from context, there appears to be little that would support such a view. And who are we to decide that Jesus didn't really mean what He said?

Before and after the Cross

When did this New Covenant begin? If you flip in your Bible to Matthew 1 and then turn back one page, what does it say in big block letters? "THE NEW TESTAMENT." Is that really where the New Covenant (the New Testament era) begins—in Matthew 1?

Actually, no.

The New Covenant begins at the death of Christ, not at His birth. We see this in various places in Scripture. First, Hebrews tells us a covenant does not take effect without a death:

> ... because a will [covenant] is in force **only when somebody has died**; it never takes effect while the one who made it is living. (Hebrews 9:17)

Even in inaugurating the Old Covenant, it was all about blood and death. Moses sprinkled blood all over the scroll and all over the people (Exodus 24:8). Now that's a church service I'm willing to miss! But God made it graphic on purpose. He wanted to show the people that without the shedding of blood, a covenant does not take effect.

Jesus said, "This is the new covenant in my blood" at the Last Supper (Luke 22:20). The New Covenant is *not* in His birth but *in His blood*. Furthermore, Galatians states that Jesus was *born under the Law* and His audience was under the Law:

> But when the set time had fully come, God sent his Son, born of a woman, **born under the law**, to redeem **those under the law**, that we might receive adoption to sonship. (Galatians 4:4–5)

The cross is the dividing line of human history. It wasn't until Jesus's death that the New Covenant went into effect.

Why is this so important? Because those impossible teachings of Jesus are easily explained, in context, once we understand that Jesus was born and lived in an era of Old Testament law, and sometimes He was simply exposing the true spirit of the Law.

The Two Messages of Jesus

Jesus didn't have just one message. He had two. First, we see "your friendly neighborhood Jesus." His mission was to teach us about the brand-new way inaugurated in His blood. These teachings include the announcement of a vine-and-branches relationship with Him, the indwelling of the Holy Spirit, and His second coming. These were "coming soon" through His death and resurrection.

But Jesus's second message should *also* be acknowledged: He sought to bury the prideful and religious by showcasing "Moses 2.0." That's exactly what the Sermon on the Mount is—It's Moses 2.0. It's the Law on steroids. It's the true spirit of what God actually demands under the Law: perfection. This is not your friendly neighborhood Jesus. This is the Lord with a sword: Cut off your hand. Pluck out your eye. Comply in every way or be in danger of the fires of Hell.

So, what if not all of Jesus's teachings are the same? What if there's a simpler, better way to understand why Jesus would teach such impossible things? What if *some* of His teachings have a totally different purpose altogether? And what if, underneath it all, there's a greater truth to realize?

With this paradigm shift, the purpose of Jesus's harshest teachings is exposed. Jesus brought frustration to all who depended on religious effort to achieve rightness with God. And He came to reveal a new way of living—one of free, full, and right standing before God. But before this new way could come into effect, Jesus had to bury His Jewish audience under the futility of their own Law-keeping efforts. If anyone thinks they can keep the Law, Jesus simply directs them to the Sermon on the Mount. If Moses kills, Moses 2.0 kills even more.

CHAPTER 17

Mount Everest has two base camps. The first one is on the north side of the mountain in Tibet. The second is on the south side in Nepal. Supplies are shipped to these camps so climbers will have everything they need for the treacherous ascent that awaits them. Climbers typically stay at one of these base camps for several days to acclimatize themselves and avoid altitude sickness before beginning their trek up Mount Everest. Tourists often visit them just to get a feel for what it's like to prepare for such an incredible climb.

Now, imagine you're one of those tourists visiting a base camp. But when you arrive, what you find there is astonishing. You encounter a group of people who arrived just ahead of you and are celebrating as if they've reached the peak of Mount Everest. The problem is that the base camp has not had a shipment of supplies in a long time, and none of the people have the right equipment or even seem particularly fit or knowledgeable about climbing. There's absolutely no way any of them would make it to the peak. They would surely die on their journey. Their celebration is delusional; in reality, they are nowhere near the top of Everest and have no real hope of getting there.

So what would you tell them? Would you be direct and honest with them about their true progress and the dangers of a climb to the actual summit? Or would you go along with the charade and pat them on the back for their so-called "accomplishment"?

This is what we see in the Sermon on the Mount. Jesus witnesses a group of Pharisees celebrating their Law-keeping, claiming to have arrived at the peak of Sinai's Law-based living. In actuality, in terms of climbing the mountain of God's righteousness, they are still at base camp.

So what did Jesus do? Did He pat them on the back and tell them they were doing great and not to worry because God would grade them on a curve?

No! What we find in the Sermon on the Mount is a very direct and honest assessment of where the Jews really were—nowhere near the pinnacle of true obedience to the Law.

The Lord with a Sword

The Sermon on the Mount begins with the Beatitudes. These are blessings or rewards for those who are meek, merciful, and pure. But we quickly find out that Jesus's definition of meek, merciful, and pure leaves *none* of His present hearers blessed or rewarded.

Jesus then introduces the topic of the Law, and here's what we see next: Jesus drives nails in the coffin of anyone who thinks they can keep the Law. He begins with a revolutionary announcement: He has not come to abolish the Law, but to fulfill it. He then proceeds to lay out, in excruciating and painful detail, the true and *impossible* standard of the Law.

Jesus's goal is to show exactly how hard it is to fulfill the Law and therefore, by implication, why He's the only person who could fulfill it. He makes it clear that none of the Law has gone away or will go away until Heaven and Earth pass away. The Law is a force to be reckoned with, and there is no getting around it. One must confront its true demands and live them out. Impossible!

Jesus emphasizes that no one should claim any of the 613 regulations within the Law have been annulled. He also makes it clear that anyone who can actually obey the Law will be called "great" in Heaven. However, we know from the Apostle Paul that no one can keep the Law (Galatians 3:10–11). Therefore, no one will actually be called great in Heaven because of their Law-keeping. Jesus is describing a set of exactly *zero* Law-keepers who will be called great in Heaven.

A quick examination of the standard shows just how impossible it is to reach: Anger equals murder? Looking with lust equals adultery? Name-calling is punished by throwing you into a fiery Hell? You're supposed to let people beat you up, sue you, and take all your belongings? The threat of Hell appears three different times in the Sermon on the Mount. Yet this same threat is never levied against believers in the writings of Peter, James, John, or Paul.

What we witness here is not "your friendly neighborhood Jesus." This is "the Lord with a sword," telling them to sever body parts or suffer the fiery consequences. Again, if we were living these teachings out today, dedicated churchgoers would hock all their belongings on eBay, and the Church itself would look like an amputation ward:

> *If **your right eye** causes you to sin, **gouge it out** and throw it away. It is better for you to lose one part of your body than for your whole body to be thrown into **hell**.* (Matthew 5:29)

> *And if **your right hand** causes you to sin, **cut it off** and throw it away. It is better for you to lose one part of your body than for your whole body to go into **hell**.* (Matthew 5:30)

Finally, while the Law allowed for making vows to the Lord, Jesus is clear that His listeners are not to make any vows. Instead, they're invited to be perfectly consistent as they say "yes" or "no" about a matter, never changing their mind or failing to fulfill a commitment (Matthew 5:33–37). How possible is that?

Are these impossible teachings of Jesus truly aimed at Christians today? Should these harsh passages be seen as standards to aspire to? Or was there an altogether different purpose for them?

Many theologians and Christian authors either overlook these questions entirely or water down the impossible teachings of Jesus to make them more palatable. What if we are to take these teachings at face value in all their impossible glory? And then, what if Jesus never expected us to be able to obey any of them?

Maybe this is precisely why Matthew 5 concludes with the command to be perfect just like God:

> **Be perfect**, *therefore,* **as your heavenly Father** *is perfect.* (Matthew 5:48)

In recognizing the Sermon on the Mount as Moses 2.0, are we then to conclude that Jesus *enjoys* pointing out their spiritual death and addiction to sin? No, on the contrary, just as the Law is "our tutor to lead us to Christ, so that we may be justified by faith" (Galatians 3:24), Jesus's ministry is one of lovingly tutoring people toward Himself.

Think about it: How will they recognize their need for Him unless He first reveals their senseless attempts at Law-based living? His listeners, who included many Pharisees and Jews who were publicly boasting about their Law-keeping, *had* to see that "by the works of the Law no flesh will be justified" (Galatians 2:16b). Until the futility of their own self-effort was revealed, there was no need to look for another way—a way the Messiah would provide through His cross and resurrection.

CHAPTER 18

As a kid, I used to read Choose Your Own Adventure books. I liked them because the reader became the protagonist in the story. After just a few pages, you'd be given different options. And from there, depending on your choice, different events would unfold. At each decision point, you'd get to determine the actions of the main character and, ultimately, the ending of the book. And if you ended up somewhere you didn't want to be, you could just go back to a previous decision and change it, no consequences or strings attached. So satisfying!

While that series was both fun and popular, it's the *exact opposite* of what we see with the Sermon on the Mount and the true spirit of the Law. The standard is impossibly high, and there's no room for picking and choosing. The result is desperation.

That was precisely the reaction Jesus was aiming to pro-
voke in His listeners. He wanted to show them that to take
any other approach to the Law would be to delude themselves.
God is not grading on a curve. The Law mercilessly con-
demns, and that's the whole point.

Why do so many Christians today think they're ready
and able to obey Jesus's version of Moses 2.0—the Law on
steroids—when Israel couldn't even handle Moses 1.0 to
begin with? Just as the Law itself kills, Jesus's iconic sermon
is indeed a real killer.

Still, the Church continues its love affair with the Ten
Commandments and the Sermon on the Mount, not realizing they're reading someone else's mail—because the
backbone of the Sermon on the Mount *is* the Old Testament Law.

Several times, Jesus quotes Moses: "You have heard that
it was said . . ." (referring to the Law) and then follows with
"But I tell you . . ." raising the bar for His audience:

> *You have heard that it was said to the people long ago,*
> *"Do not murder, and anyone who murders will be sub-*
> *ject to judgment." But I tell you that anyone who is*
> *angry with his brother will be subject to judgment.*
> (Matthew 5:21–22)

> *You have heard that it was said, "Do not commit adul-*
> *tery." But I tell you that anyone who looks at a woman*
> *lustfully has already committed adultery with her in his*
> *heart.* (Matthew 5:27–28)

You have heard that it was said, "*Love your neighbor and hate your enemy.*" *But I tell you:* *Love your enemies and pray for those who persecute you, that you may be sons of your Father in heaven.* (Matthew 5:43–45)

Each time, Jesus refers to the Old Testament Law that His audience knew well. Each time, He deliberately introduces a new standard that amplifies the Law—an impossible standard to which no one can attain. Furthermore, Jesus puts forth clear consequences for not reaching that impossible standard: judgment from God and punishment in Hell.

Some people attempt to frame the discourse in Matthew 5 as being about spiritual growth for the Christian. However, given the impossible standard, the repeated references made to the Jewish Law (for example, when Jesus warns them against hypocrisy when offering *animal sacrifices*), and the consequences levied upon the disobedient, such an interpretation does not seem plausible. It's not spiritual growth but one's eternal destiny (Heaven or Hell) that hangs in the balance in the sermon. It's clearly about whether they will enjoy a future existence as "sons of [their] Father in heaven" (verse 45) or whether they will be "thrown into hell" (verse 29).

Killer Sermon in Focus

Get right with your brother before offering your animal sacrifice? But we believers don't offer animal sacrifices. Obey or you'll answer to *the Sanhedrin*—a Jewish council from two thousand years ago? But we don't have any relationship to the

Sanhedrin. Do not be like the Gentiles? But most of us today *are* Gentiles.

So many Christians consider Jesus's words to be directly applicable to their lives today, yet the context is so clearly Jewish and Law-centered. Jesus's intent was undoubtedly to confront the Jews of His day about their hypocrisy and failure at Law-keeping.

The entire sermon in a nutshell is this: *Confront the whole Law. Disregard none of it. Looking with lust equals adultery. Anger equals murder, and name-calling deserves Hell. Amputate body parts in your fight against sin or be thrown into fiery punishment. Let people sue you, beat you up, and take your belongings. Always have excellent motives. Never act hypocritically. Don't judge anyone or you'll suffer judgment yourself. Be perfect like God.*

The only reason any one of us can pretend to endure this "killer sermon" is that we simply haven't applied our best efforts to the standard it establishes. We adopt a mentality of "Jesus didn't really mean it" and explain it all away as hyperbole. But those around Jesus clearly took Him at His word. When we water down these words of Jesus, His impossible teachings no longer act as the stumbling block they were intended to be. Instead, they're diminished to nothing more than a speed bump on the road to our own perceived spiritual self-advancement.

"All That I Commanded"

"But Jesus said to observe *all* that He commanded!" someone objects. "So, wouldn't this mean we should obey everything written in the Sermon on the Mount?"

No, that's not what Jesus meant in Matthew 28. Here's the passage in question:

> *Therefore, go and make disciples of all nations, baptizing them in the name of the Father and of the Son and of the Holy Spirit, and **teaching them to obey everything I have commanded you.** And surely, I am with you always, to the very end of the age."* (Matthew 28:19–20)

He was telling His disciples to teach everything He commanded them to teach. And they did. Newsflash: *The result of their obedience is found in their letters.* Yet not one single time do they write or teach that we should cut off our hands, or pluck out our eyes, or try to be perfect like God, or sell all our possessions. We don't see any of those harsh statements in any of the New Testament letters or in any of their sermons in Acts.

Why not? Because it was never Jesus's intention that the disciples teach such things to the New Testament Church. He simply meant they were to teach what He instructed them to teach. Again, they did, and we see the evidence of what they were teaching in the epistles they wrote.

Mission Accomplished!

Once we view the impossible teachings of Jesus in their proper contextual light, we don't have to water them down or explain them away any longer. Instead, we can take Jesus's words at face value, just as those who first heard them did.

The rich man went away sad. The Pharisees went away mad. Mission accomplished.

What was the mission? Jesus's plan was to purposefully bury His hearers under the condemnation of the Law, so they could see no way out apart from God's grace.

The Bottom Line

For you as a believer, it's as if Jesus Christ skied down Mount Sinai, earned a gold medal, hung it around your neck, and said, "Stay off that mountain. It'll kill you." The Law kills, but Jesus fulfilled the Law so you wouldn't even have to try.

PART 3

YOUR NEXT SIN WAS FORGIVEN

CHAPTER 19

Jonathan stopped by my office one evening after work. He'd called me earlier in the day to see if I'd be available to talk through something with him.

I got him a cup of coffee and we both sat down. I asked him what was on his mind.

A babysitter had introduced him to pornography at thirteen years old, he said, and from there nearly two decades of struggle with lust began. He had felt shame as far back as he could remember, but nothing seemed to help him find freedom—or enable him to stop.

"I've heard hundreds of sermons and read dozens of books on God's grace and forgiveness. But for some reason, I can't believe God is going to forgive me for my habitual pattern of sinning with porn," Jonathan said despairingly.

"Well, God's not going to forgive you," I said.

Knowing I'm a teacher of grace, he looked at me, perplexed. "What do you mean?" he asked.

"God's not *going* to forgive you," I clarified. "He already has!

"That's where you're getting tripped up," I told him. "If you're in Christ, then you're already a totally forgiven person, period. Your past, present, and future sins have been taken away, once for all. That's just a fact that you can either believe or wrestle with, but it's true either way. So, it's not really your decision to make. God already decided, and it's finished."

"Yeah, but I guess I just look at the number of times I've sinned against God. Not only that, but it's willful sin. I knew what I was doing, and I did it anyway. Isn't willful sin more serious?" Jonathan argued.

"All of our sins are willful," I said. "We can't really say, 'God, I don't know what happened. My will wasn't involved.' No, every sin is willful, and every sin is serious.

"That's why Jesus had to go to the cross," I explained, "to die for every one of our willful sins. And the cross worked. End of story. It's over! The sacrifice of Jesus was God's final act regarding your sins. He remembers your sins no more."

Jonathan looked at me. There was a glimmer of hope in his eyes, but he still couldn't quite believe it. "It's harder to agree with that when it's your own sins, when it's the failures you've managed to live with for so long," he admitted.

"Yes, I hear you," I said, "But ultimately you're going to have to decide whether or not you are somehow an exception to the finished work of Christ. You're going to have to decide which is bigger: your sins or your Savior."

"When you put it that way," Jonathan said, "it's a whole lot clearer."

I agreed; it should be clear. It should be plain and obvious that we cannot compete with the work of the cross. *We cannot out-sin the grace of Christ. The blood of Jesus never runs out!*

You cannot take God by surprise. He already saw all of your sins ahead of time and decided to take them away forever. The only worthy punishment for sin is death. Jesus died. There's no punishment left. That means you are a totally forgiven person.

We talked more about sinful thoughts, where they come from, and how to say "no" to them. But the best part was watching Jonathan walk out of my office with a perspective on the finished work of Christ that was ten times bigger than when he first walked in. He finally realized that God was for him, not against him. He believed God loved him and even liked him. Through the work of the Son, he'd seen the face of the Father.

Again and Again?

The Israelites continually offered sacrifices for their sins. The work was never done. If they'd miraculously encountered a perfect sacrifice for all sins, the whole sacrificial system could've been shut down. But this never happened. Instead, throughout history, we see them offering sacrifices for sin, over and over (Hebrews 10:1–2).

Each year, Israel celebrated the Day of Atonement with temple sacrifices for all the people:

*Moses said to Aaron, "Come to the altar and **sacrifice** your sin offering and your burnt offering and **make atonement** for yourself and the people; **sacrifice** the offering that is for the people and **make atonement** for them, as the Lord has commanded."* (Leviticus 9:7)

Three hundred and sixty-five days of sins were dealt with at one time on the Day of Atonement. But the work was never finished. Moses told Aaron to offer sacrifices, year after year. Those annual sacrifices served as a beautiful *shadow* or *symbol* of the one-time sacrifice of Jesus that would one day take place. Still, the Old Testament sacrifices never really brought cleansing to anyone (Hebrews 10:4).

Atonement versus Takeaway

Old Testament sacrifices brought more and more forgiveness once a year. Jesus brought you forgiveness once for all. Old Testament sacrifices atoned for sins. Jesus took away your sins. Old Testament sacrifices were an annual reminder of sins (Hebrews 10:3). Jesus remembers your sins no more!

Hebrews 10:3–4 says it was "impossible for the blood of bulls and goats to take away sins." I hear believers often assure each other with, "Don't worry, your sins are under the blood." However, that only implies a sin covering like Israel had under the Law. The truth is your sins are *not* "under the blood." (After all, what if one crept out the side?) No, your sins have been taken away forever. They're removed as far as the East is from the West (Psalm 103:12).

Your sins are *not* covered. They're *gone!*

This is another way the blood of Jesus is greater than the blood of bulls and goats. Old Testament sacrifices brought a temporary covering of sins. They functioned as a shadow or picture of the final sacrifice. John the Baptist realized how revolutionary and perfect the sacrifice of Jesus would be when he shouted, "Look, the Lamb of God, who *takes away* the sin of the world!" (John 1:29).

The Perfect Sacrifice

Ultimately, there *was* a perfect sacrifice for Israel: Jesus. You, too, have a perfect sacrifice in Him. His death for your sins means you can shut down all systems for getting more forgiveness and more cleansing. You can do away with your formulas for getting right and staying right with God. You can put full confidence in the once-for-all sacrifice of Christ.

This means there are no religious hoops to jump through. Instead, you're invited to rest in the one-time sacrifice of Jesus that brought you to God:

> *For Christ also **suffered once for sins**, the righteous for the unrighteous, **to bring you to God**. He was put to death in the body but made alive in the Spirit.* (1 Peter 3:18)

What Should I Do, Then?

People often ask, "If I don't need more forgiveness, then what should I do when I sin?"

Here's a crazy idea: Stop. Maybe even stop, drop, and roll. (Note: This also works well during a fire!) But seriously, what if you turned away from sin? What if you thanked God for the forgiveness you have in Christ? What if you moved forward, trusting Jesus for new attitudes and actions?

In Ephesians 4:28, Paul urges believers to stop stealing, get a job, work with their hands, and give to those in need. However, at no time are they told to ask for forgiveness. Apparently, they can *thank* God for that!

Yes, you seek peace with others when you've sinned against them (Romans 12:18; James 5:16). But that's peace with *others*. You already have peace with God through Jesus (Romans 5:1). You make peace with others, because they didn't die for your sins. But you don't need to seek peace with God. He took your sins away forever and holds none of them against you (Romans 4:8; 1 Corinthians 13:5).

The Bottom Line

There are plenty of reasons for you to turn from sin, but getting more forgiveness is *not* one of those reasons. There's nothing you can do to make yourself more forgiven than you are at this moment. If you're in Christ, you're a totally forgiven person, once and for all time (Hebrews 10:14).

CHAPTER 20

I've spent a lot of time in Europe—Spain and Italy in particular. I've seen beautiful landscapes, met wonderful people, and eaten amazing food. But there's one aspect of my travels I've found to be heartbreaking.

Nearly anywhere I've gone in Spain and Italy, there's been a cathedral. And inside those edifices, I've seen things that make me both cringe and cry. Often, they feel more like graveyards than churches.

With the exception of Easter, there's little to no recognition of the risen Christ. Many people are kneeling, some with their heads on the floor, appealing to a statue of Jesus (still!) on the cross, or Mary, or a "saint." They're seeking God's favor. And when it comes to forgiveness, they're always needing more and more, and the desperation shows. There's no joy, only guilt and despair, as they confess their sins and take communion again and again. They believe each act of contrition brings forgiveness only for those sins, and they'll need to be back soon to obtain more cleansing.

The once-for-all forgiveness found in Jesus seems to be a foreign concept altogether. But they're not alone in that regard. Here in the United States, it sometimes feels like Protestants are just as confused. On one hand, we say we're totally forgiven. On the other hand, we're constantly asking God for more: more forgiveness, more cleansing, more grace, more, more, more.

Once-for-All Forgiveness

In 2017, I sat in my living room as a friend tried to sell me on an idea called "Bitcoin." A digital currency operating independently of any central bank? The whole idea sounded stupid to me. It's been several years since that day, and I have to ask: Who's stupid now? If I had made even a fraction of the investment my friend was suggesting, I would've made millions of dollars (or at least thousands before I sold too early!). I just couldn't bring myself to embrace such an unusual currency.

To understand this once-for-all forgiveness, we need to embrace another unusual currency: God's blood currency. Hebrews 9:22 says "without the shedding of blood there is no forgiveness." We are totally forgiven because of blood, not apologies.

In our human relationships, we're used to a word-based currency for forgiveness. You forgive me when I show up on your doorstep with an apology on my lips and sorrow in my heart. And of course, tears in my eyes would be a real bonus. This is how we humans operate.

We have an apology-based economy for sins. But God has a blood-based economy for sins.

This is why, for thousands of years, Israel was commanded to offer blood sacrifices. At the inauguration of the Law, animals were killed, and blood was sprinkled over the scroll and all over the people. Now, that's when you don't want to forget your umbrella for church! Through this graphic display, God was trying to tell them something important about blood and forgiveness.

At the Day of Atonement, the Jews were not required to name or even remember every sin committed over the past year. How could they? Instead, they relied on the blood of bulls and goats as the covering for their sins. It was never about their memory and words. It was always about the blood.

Likewise, for us today, it's about the blood of Jesus. But here's the difference: Jesus shed His blood only once. It worked the first time. No repeat needed. Because of His one-time blood sacrifice, you're as forgiven today as you'll ever be. Did you catch that? There's nothing you can do to be more forgiven than you already are!

Imagine if you were only forgiven for the sins you asked forgiveness for. What if you forgot one? The truth is that you've already forgotten about thousands of times you've sinned. So, what if you passed away with all those uncon-fessed sins? This is why it can't be about your memory, your legal pad, and your constant confessions. It must be about the blood of Christ, and it is finished.

The Sin Issue Is Over!

The fact that Jesus died on the cross only *once* is taken for granted: "Well, duh? What did you expect?" But to the Jews, a one-time sacrifice with no further death needed means something powerful.

Here's what it means: Jesus is not up in Heaven hanging on a cross over and over, so you're not down here on Earth being forgiven over and over.

> *Unlike the other high priests, **he does not need to offer sacrifices day after day**, first for his own sins, and then for the sins of the people. He sacrificed for their sins **once for all** when he offered himself.* (Hebrews 7:27)

> *Nor did he enter heaven to offer himself again and again, the way the high priest enters the Most Holy Place every year with blood that is not his own. **Otherwise Christ would have had to suffer many times** since the creation of the world. But he has appeared **once for all** at the culmination of the ages to do away with sin by the sacrifice of himself.* (Hebrews 9:25–26)

Jesus isn't dying day after day, or again and again. And God wants you to see the importance of this:

- Only blood brings forgiveness.
- Jesus shed His blood two thousand years ago.
- He'll never shed His blood again.
- You're as forgiven right now as you'll ever be.

Once a Jewish person came to know total forgiveness in Jesus, his or her Law-based efforts at staying cleansed before God could cease. Going back to the Temple for more forgiveness made no sense. By the same token, once you've seen what Jesus has done in making you forgiven once and for all, you can abandon the mental gymnastics of trying to become more forgiven. You can jettison the religious pursuit of trying to "get right with God" and get on His good side over and over again.

Hebrews 6 and 10 warn the Jews not to go back to temple sacrifices after hearing the message of Jesus. There's no hope and no forgiveness outside of Him. In the same way, God is urging you to put your full confidence in the finished work of Christ and not return to the religious doublemindedness you see being pushed today.

Sure, we're not killing animals for our sins in our backyards. But it's just as insulting to Jesus when we believe and teach that Christians are forgiven "positionally" but not actually. And we are insulting Jesus when we believe and teach that Christians need to ask daily for the once-for-all forgiveness we already have in Christ.

The Bottom Line

God never motivates you by withholding His forgiveness. He never holds it for ransom to get you to behave. You don't need to beg or plead with Him to forgive you. If you're in Christ, forgiveness is something you have, not something you're getting.

Jesus is not in Heaven dying every day, so you're not on Earth being forgiven every day. You aren't forgiven progressively or in installments. Jesus has already given you all the forgiveness you'll ever need.

You're a totally forgiven person, period.

CHAPTER 21

Wanda had come to me for counseling. Something had been bothering her for years, even decades.

A long time ago, she'd made a split-second mistake. While driving down the road, she didn't notice the light had turned red, and she went right through it.

Her moment of inattention resulted in the worst consequence you could imagine: she hit another car. The driver, an elderly man, went into a coma and eventually died. Without intending to, Wanda had killed someone.

She hadn't been intoxicated or on her phone, and she had a good driving record, so she didn't go to jail. Instead, she was charged with reckless driving, had to pay a large fine, and gave up her driver's license. But that hardly mattered to her compared to the responsibility she felt for what she'd done.

"Why was I the one to survive? I wish I hadn't," Wanda said. "I wish I had died that day too. I deserved to."

I was horrified as she continued, "I really wish I were dead. I've even tried a few times, but no luck so far."

"What do you mean?!" I asked.

"I've done things to try to end my life. I've taken pills, I've sat in the car in the garage with the motor running, but I couldn't even do that right," she explained.

I began to realize how serious of a situation this really was. "Have you ever talked to anyone else about this?" I asked.

"I've been to counselors and psychologists, and they've even prescribed things for me, but it all just makes me feel numb inside. I don't feel like I'm dealing with the root problem, whatever it is," she said.

I thought about what she'd shared, what she was feeling, and what I knew about God's forgiveness.

"I think the root problem is that you're disagreeing with God," I said.

"Disagreeing with God?" she asked, surprised. She hadn't heard that from the counselors she'd seen before.

"Yes, what you experienced was an accident," I explained. "You didn't intend for anyone to die. That's clear. But here's the thing: Even if what you did were intentional—which it was not—God still says you're forgiven, holy, and blameless.

"No matter what your track record, God doesn't blame you," I continued. "He says you're *blameless*. So, you need to decide whether God is right about you. You need to decide whether you want to continue seeing yourself in a way that God disagrees with.

"If not, then it's time to change your mind. You can choose to forgive yourself and recognize you are perfectly righteous apart from what happened that day. You're not the sum total of what you've done. You're the sum total of what He's done."

Wanda seemed stunned. "I've heard the word 'righteous' all my life," she said, "but I never would have seen righteousness as the answer to my problem. And, of course, I've known about forgiveness all along as well, but forgiving myself is not something I thought I could do."

"Forgiveness and righteousness are actually the answers to most problems," I replied. "You'd be surprised."

I went on to lead Wanda through the process of agreeing with God and forgiving herself. I also shared some verses with her about her righteousness. We met a few more times after that, but eventually she didn't need to talk with me anymore. Once she learned the truth about her perfect purity and rightness in Jesus, she began to relax in it. Once again, the message of God's grace had made all the difference.

Sitting Down with Jesus

A chair was a forbidden piece of furniture in the Jewish temple. Old Testament priests could never sit down on the job. God didn't allow it. He wanted the Israelites to know their forgiveness was never fully accomplished. There was always unfinished business to attend to.

*Day after day every priest **stands** and performs his religious duties; again and again he offers the same sacrifices, which can never take away sins. **But when this priest*** *had offered for all time one sacrifice for sins, he sat down at the right hand of God.* (Hebrews 10:11–12)

Notice the contrast. In the Old Testament, every priest had to stand up. Their work was never done. Day after day, they had to offer the same sacrifices which could never take away sins. But Jesus offered one sacrifice for all time and then sat down.

Jesus did the unthinkable. He did the illegal. He did what no other priest before Him could do. He sat down because it was finished.

*After [Jesus] had provided purification for sins, **he sat down** at the right hand of the Majesty in heaven.* (Hebrews 1:3b)

Did you know God is inviting you to sit down with Jesus? He wants you to agree that the once-for-all sacrifice of Christ was enough. You're forgiven completely and forever. The sin issue between you and God is over, so you can relax and enjoy.

*For **by one offering** he has **perfected for all time** those who are sanctified.* (Hebrews 10:14 NASB)

God looked down the timeline of your sins—past, present, and future—and He took them all away. The sacrifice of Jesus was a smashing success, and for that reason He sat down and relaxed concerning your forgiveness. That means you can relax too.

So what are you doing about your sins? Are you standing up, running around Planet Earth, trying to get forgiven and stay forgiven? Or are you seated with Jesus, agreeing with God that nothing else needs to be done for your forgiveness?

We believers seem to be big on "imitating Christ." So how about we imitate His satisfaction with the cross? Hebrews 10 says He perfected you for all time by one sacrifice. Would you imitate Christ by saying the same thing He says about you— that you're perfectly forgiven for all time?

Future Sins Are All in the Past!

Consider this: How many of your sins were still in the future when Jesus died? All of them, right? Yes, all of them. The sins you committed before and after salvation were all in the future. Even the sins you haven't thought of committing yet were in the future when Christ died. God made no distinction in taking them all away.

They're all the same to Him, and the blood of Jesus was the satisfying sacrifice for every single one. So if you're in Christ, you're a totally forgiven person, period. Even your next sin is already forgiven. (But hey, don't go getting any ideas! Okay, I trust you.)

This is why our forgiveness is expressed in past tense. Colossians 2:13 says He *forgave* us all our sins, past tense. Ephesians 4:32 says God *forgave* you, past tense. Hebrews 10:18 says your sins *have been* forgiven, past tense. There's a reason all of these are expressed in the past tense. Jesus has nothing left to do about your sins. You've been forgiven, and you live in a permanent state of total forgiveness.

Will Be Forgiven?

If we're totally forgiven, once for all, then why does James 5:15 say "if they have sinned, they *will be* forgiven"? That's future tense, so what's the deal?

Here, the only condition is that the sins have to be committed. In other words, they have to exist. The purpose of this passage is to comfort believers. It's a hypothetical situation, and James is assuring them that if any sins are committed, they're forgiven.

When are they forgiven? When they're committed.

We are time-based creatures. We live with the concept of past, present, and future. Here, James is simply saying that in a hypothetical future where sins are committed, they're forgiven. Because of the finished work of the cross, forgiveness of any future sin is never in doubt.

The Bottom Line

No one is 53 percent forgiven. You're either in Adam and entirely unforgiven, or you're in Christ and completely forgiven. There's no middle ground.

There's a reason it's called "the finished work of Christ"—because you don't have to finish it!

CHAPTER 22

Lucas's parents asked if I would talk to their son. He'd been struggling with disturbing sexual thoughts for some time. They'd done their best to help, but nothing seemed to make any difference.

"I've been dealing with this for almost a year. I've asked God for forgiveness probably a thousand times, and I feel nothing," Lucas exclaimed, "Aren't you supposed to *feel* something?"

He and his parents looked at me intently and waited for my answer.

"The first thing you need to know is that it's not a sin to get a thought," I said. "We all get lots of sinful thoughts offered to us. What matters is how we respond to them. But simply having the thought go through your mind is not a sin."

"Maybe not, but I've definitely done things I shouldn't, too. So, when is it a sin and when isn't it a sin?" he asked, looking for clarity.

"Unfortunately, I can't rewind through your life and tell you what was and what wasn't a sin in each instance. I'm not sure what that would do for you anyway," I said. "Even if you did know exactly how many times you sinned, the solution would still be the same."

"But I would know how to ask for forgiveness for each one, if I knew which were sins and which weren't," he argued.

"That's not how it works, Lucas," I explained. "You can't possibly remember all the sins you've committed in your life. You've already forgotten about thousands or millions of them. That's why God had to take away all your sins at one time through the cross."

"But what about apologizing to God and keeping my heart right with Him? That's what I've been told," Lucas said, wondering how it fit in with everything he'd been trying to do.

"Are you sorry for all the times you've sinned, Lucas?" I asked.

"Yes, I am," he responded without hesitation.

"And do you think God knows that? Does He know your heart?" I asked.

"Yes," Lucas answered confidently.

"Then what if it's not about having to comb through your track record to apologize for each sin and ask for forgiveness?" I asked. "Remember that all your sins were in the future when Christ died. He took them away once for all.

"It's not about you keeping short accounts with God to stay in right relationship with Him through your apologies," I explained, "God knew you could never do it. So instead, He forgave you once for all time, and He gave you a repentant heart that doesn't like sin anyway.

"God knows you. He knows you regret sin. He also knows you're a totally forgiven person. Otherwise, think about it: You couldn't even go to Heaven. Partially forgiven people don't belong in a perfect Heaven. But you're not partially forgiven. You're totally forgiven forever because of Jesus's blood—not your apologies."

"So, I don't have to ask for each sin to be forgiven?" Lucas asked again, just to make sure. He understood what I was saying, but it sounded too good to be true.

"That's right. You can't even remember them all, right?" I asked.

He nodded.

"Thank God you're forgiven—past, present, and future," I told him. "Yes, you regret sin. Yes, you ask God for wisdom moving forward. Yes, you trust Jesus with your behavior the next time. But you can't get more forgiven than you already are. The blood of Jesus cleansed you once and for all time."

I could see Lucas's shoulders drop as the relief set in. For nearly a year, he'd been wondering what to do about his mounting list of sins. Ever since he'd heard the "keep short accounts" teaching, he had been in bondage. He could finally see that God does not take his sins into account at all, and the truth set him free!

The Mathematics of Sin

How many sins have you committed in your life? Thousands? Millions? Now, how many of those have you remembered to confess and ask forgiveness for? Ouch. Not nearly as many on that second list as the first, right?

This is exactly why your forgiveness can't be about your memory and your words. Instead, it's about His cross and His blood.

You've already forgotten to confess a majority of the sins you've committed in your life. If it were about your keeping short accounts with God, it's already way too late.

Now, some have tried to "solve" this problem by saying God doesn't worry about the sins we've forgotten about. So, if we forget, He forgets? If that were true, the best plan would be to just load up on Benadryl until Christ returns. Maybe if we go through life in a comatose state with spiritual amnesia, then apparently God forgets our sins too, and the problem is solved? This line of thinking (that God overlooks our forgetfulness in confession) is nothing but conjecture and is not supported by Scripture.

The real solution to your millions of unconfessed sins is that it's not about you anyway. It's about Jesus. Your forgiveness is through Him and what He accomplished on Calvary, not through your daily (or hourly!) confessions or asking for forgiveness.

Romans 4:8 says God does not take your sins into account. How can it be about short accounts if God doesn't take your sins into account? You're not asked to keep short accounts, because there's no account. God destroyed the record book!

Is It Appropriate to "Appropriate"?

Maybe you've heard you're totally forgiven—past, present, and future—but you just need to *appropriate* it daily. Who knows what that means?

Somebody says, "Well, it means to make true in your own experience what God has done for you eternally." Make true? How do you "make true" the forgiveness you already have in Jesus? It's *already* true. To demonstrate the foolishness of this, go ahead and appropriate your forgiveness right now.

Yes, take a minute right now. We've got time.

Okay, now that you're back, how did it go? Do you see my point? How do you know when you've "appropriated" it? Is being forgiven a feeling? An experience? It seems to me that being forgiven is a fact that is true because of the cross. You're just forgiven, period.

Yes, it's really that simple.

The Catholic Claim

Catholic doctrine agrees that forgiveness only comes by blood. That's why they have Jesus dying over and over again at the Lord's Supper. It's called *transubstantiation*. As they attend mass and take the bread and wine, they think Jesus is hanging on the cross again and again. They believe He sheds His blood more and more.

At least they've got one thing right: "without the shedding of blood there is no forgiveness" (Hebrews 9:22). Where they go wrong is in claiming the bloodshed is *ongoing*. Hebrews works hard to convince us that Jesus died once and will never die again. He's not up in Heaven dying over and over, so you're not down here on Earth being forgiven over and over again.

> *Nor did he enter heaven to offer himself again and again*, *the way the high priest enters the Most Holy Place every year with blood that is not his own.* *Otherwise Christ would have had to suffer many times* *since the creation of the world. But he has appeared* *once for all* *at the culmination of the ages* *to do away with sin* *by the sacrifice of himself. Just as people are destined to die once, and after that to face judgment,* *so Christ was sacrificed once to take away the sins of many;* *and he will appear a second time, not to bear sin, but to bring salvation to those who are waiting for him.* (Hebrews 9:25–28)

> *Then he adds: "Their sins and lawless acts I will remember no more." And where these have been forgiven,* *sacrifice for sin is no longer necessary.* (Hebrews 10:17–18)

You Don't Have to Ask or Wonder!

It's by blood alone—and the bloodshed is over, so it's finished. This is why we see the phrase "ask forgiveness" or "ask for forgiveness" exactly *zero* times in the New Testament letters. We're never called to ask for what we already have in Christ. That would be like asking Jesus to die over and over again each time we sin—something He'll never do.

Now you may have heard the claim, "We're *positionally* forgiven in God's heavenly bookkeeping but *not experientially* forgiven yet here on Earth."

I don't know what to say to this except: Nonsense! The terms *positional* and *experiential* are not in the New Testament. They're instances where we've looked to academia to overcomplicate the Gospel.

The Bottom Line

The reality is the Jews felt better right here (experientially!) on Planet Earth about their sins after they offered animal sacrifices. So how much more can you feel better about your sins right here and right now because of the one-time sacrifice of Jesus? Your total forgiveness is not just "positional." Your total forgiveness is reality, plain and simple.

First John 2:2 says Jesus is the *hilasterion* (propitiation)—the satisfying sacrifice. The Father is satisfied in every way with His Son's finished work. If the God of the Universe is satisfied with the sacrifice of Jesus, who are you to disagree with Him?

CHAPTER 23

Leo from Florida called in to the radio program one night.
"I truly hunger and thirst for God," he said, "but I still struggle with sin."

"I know I'm going to Heaven, and I know I'm saved," he continued. "But some people tell me I have to repent of each sin in order to be forgiven. They say you sin every day, and therefore you've got to repent every day of each one, or you're not getting right before God."

Here's what I shared with Leo and with others who've been confused by the issue of repentance and forgiveness. The idea that we have to keep "short accounts" with God is a very common teaching. This misunderstanding causes masses of people to misconstrue the grace of God. They end up believing they're forgiven of all their sins . . . unless they sin. They're forgiven of all their sins unless they commit one. Then it's up to them to get more forgiven. That's absurd, and it's not the Gospel.

There are many reasons to turn away from sin daily, but getting more forgiveness is not one of those reasons. We turn from sin—not to find more forgiveness from God, but to find more contentment in God. So let's be honest about how horrible sin is, but let's also be honest about how forgiven we believers are.

Should we turn from sin? Of course. Get away from sin? Absolutely. How often? Every single time. Why? To get more forgiven by God? No. You're already as forgiven today as you'll ever be. We do it because it's not who we are. We are dead to sin and not made for it anymore. We are alive to God, and sin is beneath us.

Can you be forgiven and miserable at the same time? For sure. So that's the reason to stop sinning—not to get more forgiven but to find more fulfillment.

Consider the man in Corinth who was having inappropriate relations with his father's wife. There was church discipline for him, since he was asked to leave. He didn't care what the church congregation thought, anyway. He was rebelling, so Paul said to remove him. Was he forgiven? Yes, but he was also miserable. In fact, he was so miserable that by the time we find out more about him in 2 Corinthians, he has come to his senses, repented, and returned to the church. And Paul is instructing the church to receive him so that he doesn't experience "excessive sorrow" (2 Corinthians 2:7).

Repentance versus Asking for Forgiveness

Repentance and asking for forgiveness are two different things. Repentance means to turn away from something and to believe or act differently. Obviously, we believers are called to turn from sinful ideas every single time.

That's a no-brainer!

But "asking for forgiveness" is entirely different. It assumes we're not yet forgiven. So, we need to ask God to swoop down out of Heaven and bring us a new portion of cleansing for our most recent sin, and then for the next sin, and the next one.

This is simply *not* biblical.

The idea of asking God for forgiveness is pervasive in the religions of the world. But not one single time in any New Testament epistle are we told to ask God for forgiveness. While the idea of asking for forgiveness is very religious, it's just not Jesus. Turn from sin? Yes, every time. But why would you *ask* God for something you already have?

In both Ephesians and Colossians, we're told that in Him we have redemption, the forgiveness of sins (Ephesians 1:7; Colossians 1:14). Redemption and forgiveness of sins are something you have, not something you are getting. You were redeemed and forgiven at the same time. You have both in Jesus at the very moment you were placed in Him.

You don't wake up every day and ask for redemption. You don't cry out each morning, "Lord, please redeem me! Please buy me back!" Why not? Because you've already been redeemed. You were bought for a price, and you are now a person of God's possession. You would not ask to be redeemed over and over again.

So, why are you asking to be forgiven every day? Redemption and forgiveness are one and the same. You received both at salvation when you were placed in Christ.

It was a package deal.

Thoughts on Confession

The word *confess* means "to agree." Shouldn't we agree with God about everything? Yes, we confess that He created the world. We confess that Jesus is Lord. We confess that cheating on our spouse or our taxes is sin. We agree with God about everything, but we don't do it to get more forgiveness.

All of the forgiveness we'll ever need for a lifetime and eternity was provided through the cross. Our forgiveness is not contingent upon daily confessions. Our forgiveness rests entirely on the finished work of the cross.

One person goes to a priest regularly to confess his sins, thinking that's how he gets forgiven by God. Another chuckles at the idea of a human priest and instead goes to God directly, asking Him for forgiveness and cleansing each day.

Both people are in error.

Why? Because both ignore the finished work of Christ. Any system, whether Catholic, Protestant, or other, that doesn't factor in the finished work of Christ is flawed from the start. There's no system of any kind for getting more forgiveness and cleansing. It's all or nothing. We're either in Adam, unforgiven, or we are in Christ, totally forgiven for all time (Hebrews 10:14). There's nothing in between: *No one on the planet is partially forgiven.*

What about confessing our sin struggles to other people? James writes, "Therefore confess your sins to each other and pray for each other so that you may be healed. The prayer of a righteous person is powerful and effective" (James 5:16). This is about sharing your struggles with trusted friends and asking them to pray for you. It has nothing to do with getting more forgiveness from God. You're designed to live in community with other believers and share struggles with them. But sharing your struggles doesn't make you more forgiven by God. It simply makes you more prayed-for by friends.

In short, let's be candid about struggles with sin, but let's also be candid about once-for-all forgiveness in Jesus.

The Bottom Line

You may be tempted to think your sins are so big, but the Bible was written by murderers. Moses killed an Egyptian in rage, and he wrote the first five books of the Bible. David put a guy on the front lines of his army to ensure his death so David could take his wife. (That was not nice!) And David wrote the Psalms. The Apostle Paul stood by and gave hearty approval at the stoning of Stephen. He was an assassin and led the massacre of the early Church. Paul wrote more New Testament letters than anyone else. So, yes, the Bible was written by murderers.

No matter how big you think your sins are, God is so much bigger. And He has qualified you through Jesus Christ. So, are you obsessed with the size of your sins? Or will you be obsessed with the size of your Savior?

CHAPTER 24

I was having a talk with Rich after one of our Wednesday night Bible studies. It was a beautiful spring evening in West Texas, with no dust storm like the ones we sometimes get that make it impossible to sit outside.

On one side of the church, we have a covered patio with picnic tables. When the weather is nice, we eat meals together there. Rich had been going to our church for about a year. He had some questions, and this one had been bothering him for a while.

"I get what you're saying about us being forgiven of all sins," Rich said, "but the one thing I can't figure out is this: What about 1 John 1:9?"

He'd been told in Bible college that we confess our sins and appropriate the truth of 1 John 1:9 to remain "experientially" forgiven and cleansed by God. He'd been taught that the

Apostle John is showing believers how to maintain cleansing before God so we can remain in daily relationship with Him.

"That sounds good, Rich," I said, "until we actually try to put it into practice. I still haven't met the person that is first-John-one-nining without missing any sins."

"But don't you agree that John says to confess our sins in order to be forgiven and cleansed?" Rich asked. "After all, it's right there in the Bible."

"Yes, John definitely wrote that," I said. "But the question is: Whom is he addressing? And in context, you might be surprised."

"What do you mean?" Rich inquired curiously.

I explained that while John is telling his readers they need to admit their sins, it was because some had never done that. That's right, some weren't even believers. They had never admitted their sinfulness—which is the first step to accepting Christ. One has to admit he or she needs a Savior.

In early Church times, people were denying they'd ever sinned. John was inviting sin-deniers to come to their senses and admit their need for Jesus. Then they'd be forgiven and cleansed of all sins. But as a believer, I told Rich, you've already done that. You admitted you were a sinner at salvation.

"Okay, I get what you're saying. You're saying the passage is addressing unbelievers. I've actually heard that before, but isn't the letter written to believers? In fact, the whole New Testament is written to churches!" Rich said, confused.

"Rich, are we to believe that Peter, James, John, and Paul never evangelized in their letters? Are we to believe they never clarified false doctrines, heresies, so that more would believe in Christ and be saved? Surely, they had evangelistic hearts, didn't they?" I asked.

Rich thought about it for a few moments and admitted, "Yes, I see what you're saying . . . but how do we know this is one of those times when John was evangelizing?"

"This is one of the obvious times, Rich," I said. "Just look at surrounding verses. John is politely saying, 'If we think we've never sinned, and if we say we have no sin, we're making God a liar, and the truth is not in us. So, if that's the case for any of us, let's go ahead and admit our sinfulness so we can be forgiven of all our sins.'"

"Yeah, but how do we know that's an unbeliever he's talking to? I just don't get it." Rich said.

I explained again, "Can you be a believer and say you've never sinned a day in your life?"

"No," Rich agreed.

"Exactly," I said. "So, who must he be talking to, then?"

Rich looked thoughtful. "That's definitely not what I grew up believing and not what I was taught, but I'll think about it and look at it again," he said.

"Absolutely, read the chapter again with this in mind and see what you think," I replied.

No Daily Bar of Soap

First John 1:9 begins with a big "IF." It says, "If we confess our sins, he is faithful and just and will forgive us our sins and purify us from all unrighteousness" (1 John 1:9).

This passage has often been used to comfort people struggling with sin. The comforting words go something like this:

"I'm sorry you're struggling. But rest assured that if you confess your sins, God will forgive you. That's His promise."

While this may sound like good, comforting advice, we should confront this reality: *What if I don't confess one? What if I can't remember them all? What if I leave one out?*

The "comforting promise" above doesn't really reflect the finished work of Christ. We should be telling a believer who is struggling that God has *already* forgiven them. The sin issue between them and God is over. We can encourage them to thank God (not ask Him!) for the forgiveness they now enjoy because of the blood of Jesus. They don't need to try to get what they've already got.

Think about it. If 1 John 1:9 is written to Christians as a bar of soap for daily cleansing, there's one *logical* problem: You've committed millions of sins but only confessed thousands. Even a mobile app can't help you keep track now—it's too late! So what will happen now that you have a vast number of unconfessed sins you can't remember?

First John 1:9 is not inviting you to pull out your legal pad and begin your tabulation of sins. You don't have to obsessively confess each one, trying not to leave any out for fear of being unforgiven. No, the context of 1 John 1:9 reveals a simpler meaning that fits perfectly with the finished work of the cross.

First John 1:9 is a one-of-a-kind verse. There's no other passage in the New Testament epistles that puts a conditional "if" on God's forgiveness. This is interesting, to say the least, because if 1 John 1:9 were actually a formula for everyday forgiveness, then nearly all the New Testament churches were clueless about it. If confession were the way for Christians to get forgiven and stay forgiven regularly, it's shocking that the

Romans and the Philippians and the Corinthians and so many early church congregations were never told about it. But the plain truth is no such formula or system for daily forgiveness is found in the New Testament letters.

With this in mind, let's examine what 1 John 1:9 is really saying.

The Physicality of Jesus

At the beginning of the chapter, we see that John is highlighting the *physicality* of Jesus. But why? An early form of Gnostic heresy claimed God would never stoop so low as to come in human form. These early heretics taught that Jesus did not have a physical body. This is why John says in his fourth chapter that anyone who claims Jesus did not come in the flesh is not from God (1 John 4:3).

Part of John's agenda in writing the epistle was to fight against this heretical Gnostic claim. What we see in John's first chapter is exactly that:

> *That which was from the beginning, which we have **heard**, which we have **seen** with our eyes, which we have **looked at** and our hands have **touched**—this we proclaim concerning the Word of life. The life appeared; we have **seen** it and testify to it, and we proclaim to you the eternal life, which was with the Father and has appeared to us. We proclaim to you what we have **seen** and **heard**, so that you also may have fellowship with us. And our fellowship is with the Father and with his Son, Jesus Christ.* (1 John 1:1–3)

John uses words like *heard* and *seen* and *looked at* and *touched* to emphasize the physicality of Jesus. He does this to combat the Gnostic heresy that Jesus was not physical.

The Reality of Sin

Why is this important to understand? Because shortly after, in the same chapter, John combats a *second* Gnostic heresy. He fights against the idea that sin is not real: "If we claim to be without sin, we deceive ourselves and the truth is not in us" (1 John 1:8). He also writes, "If we claim we have not sinned, we make him out to be a liar and his word is not in us" (1 John 1:10).

The Gnostics denied the physicality of Jesus and the reality of sin. John's first chapter fights *both* Gnostic heresies. And 1 John 1:9 is simply an invitation to the Gnostic sin-denier to come to his senses and admit his sinfulness. If he will do so, he can be saved, which results in forgiveness and the cleansing of *all* unrighteousness.

Notice the word "all" in verse 9. This is not about one-by-one forgiveness from God. No, this is about a Gnostic sin-denier agreeing with God about his sinfulness in order to obtain total forgiveness in Jesus.

Some argue that John is referring to believers because he uses the word "we" in verse 9. But John uses the word "we" throughout the passage to refer to both believers and unbelievers. In this way, he politely fights against the Gnostic heresy with a series of "if we" statements:

Verse 6	if we claim to have fellowship yet walk in darkness	unbeliever
Verse 7	if we walk in the light, the blood purifies us from all sin	believer
Verse 8	if we claim to be without sin, truth is not in us	unbeliever
Verse 9	if we confess our sins, He will forgive and cleanse of all	evangelistic
Verse 10	if we say that we have not sinned, His word is not in us	unbeliever

The word "we" is used interchangeably for humans who are in darkness and humans who are in the light. And the word "we" is used interchangeably for those who are forgiven of all sins versus those who still won't admit their sins. With John's alternating use of "we" (referring to we humans), he's saying: "If the shoe fits us, wear it!"

The Bottom Line

Imagine I introduce you to a friend this way: "Meet my friend, Jim. Jim is currently walking in darkness and claims to be without sin. Jim says he has never sinned a day in his life, and the truth of God's Word is not in Jim."

Do you walk away from meeting Jim concluding he's a believer? Certainly not! Jim is not even ready to say he has a sin problem, much less admit his need for a Savior.

This is the true meaning of 1 John 1:9. And it reveals the evangelistic heart of John. John wants to persuade people like Jim to stop entertaining the fantasy of sinless perfection and recognize Jesus died for good reason—to forgive them of the many sins they've committed.

After all, what is the first step to becoming a believer? Agreeing with God, "Lord, I'm a sinner." The Gnostic sin-deniers of John's day were not ready to assert this. So John wanted to open their eyes. He begged them to admit their sinfulness and find total forgiveness and cleansing in Christ.

This is the true meaning of 1 John 1:9. It's not a bar of soap for daily cleansing. So why are we misapplying it? Why are we putting conditions on a believer's forgiveness? Why are we disrespecting the finished work of Jesus Christ?

Let's agree with God about everything, including that we've sinned. But let's also agree with Him that we've been forgiven for our sins—past, present, and future—for all time (Hebrews 10:14).

CHAPTER 25

Brenda sent me an email asking about fellowship with God and sin.

"I go to a church where they teach you're out of fellowship with God if you sin," she wrote. "You must confess your sins and ask for God's forgiveness in order to get back in fellowship. If you don't, I've learned you could even fall out of fellowship with God permanently.

"Mainly, I'd like to know what you say about us losing fellowship with God if we have unconfessed sins," she concluded. "Is what we're being taught right?"

I've received hundreds of emails like Brenda's over the years. A lot of people are confused about fellowship with God. They believe confessing each and every sin maintains their cleansed status before God. If they fail to confess one, they'll fall out of fellowship with God. Then, some believe, God doesn't hear or answer their prayers.

Falling Out of Fellowship?

The word "fellowship" is never used that way in the New Testament. You're either in fellowship with God and have total forgiveness, or you are out of fellowship with God and still dead in your sins. There's no bouncing in and out of fellowship based on your recent track record. Sure, there are consequences for the choices you make—and we'll review those here too—but you're always in fellowship with God.

Throughout the New Testament, you see the promises of God concerning His presence in your life. He'll never leave you nor forsake you (Hebrews 13:5). Even when you're faithless, He remains faithful (2 Timothy 2:13). No one can snatch you out of His hand (John 10:28). Nothing separates you from the love of Christ (Romans 8:38).

Your fellowship with God is unshakeable and unbreakable.

If you're going to choose sin, you have to do so while you're in fellowship with God. In fact, it's God's presence within you that inspires you to express godly sorrow when you sin (2 Corinthians 7:10). If God revoked His presence every time you stumbled, you would never find your way out of temptation. It's the fact that you're new-hearted and one spirit with the Lord that empowers you to say "no" to sin and "yes" to who you truly are—a child of God in fellowship with your Father.

Watering Down the Wages

Remember: The wages of sin is death, not being out of fellowship for fifteen minutes. That would be watering down the wages. Jesus died. He paid the wages. There are no wages left. You'll never die for your sins. Jesus died for them already. So, we have no business inventing lesser punishments from God for sin. If God wanted to punish you for sin, it would be death. But He's never going to do that. There's no condemnation for you, ever (Romans 8:1).

The word *fellowship* appears over ten times in the New Testament. We learn a believer is in fellowship with God and with other Christians, while an unbeliever is not. We never see a believer going in and out of fellowship in the New Testament. We are either in fellowship (saved) or out of fellowship (lost). There is no middle ground.

Think about it: What's the only thing that would make God angry with you? Sins. Well, what did Jesus do with your sins? He took them away forever.

When You Sin . . .

Believers have fellowship with the Father and the Son and the Holy Spirit (1 Corinthians 1:9; 2 Corinthians 13:14; Philippians 2:1) and with other believers (1 John 1:3, 7). Our bond with Jesus is strong and secure. We are one spirit with the Lord (1 Corinthians 6:17).

Yes, there are earthly consequences to our sinful choices. Sin can affect our marriage, our children, or our job. And yes, we sometimes grieve (Ephesians 4:30) or quench (1 Thessalonians 5:19) the Spirit by resisting His counsel. Remember that grieving the Spirit means He is deeply concerned over us (not angry), and quenching the Spirit means we're not expressing Him. Still, none of this changes our "fellowship" with God. Sure, it changes our level of contentment and fulfillment. It also changes how much we are reflecting Christ to others. But it doesn't alter what the Bible calls "fellowship"—our bond of relationship with God. He never leaves us, and He never changes what He feels about us (Hebrews 13:5; 1 Corinthians 13:5).

So when we choose sin, we do so while we're in fellowship with Christ. That's why sinning is not as fun anymore! Have you noticed? Your neighbor may sit around fantasizing about new ways to sin, but you're wanting to avoid sin. You're different. You're an alien and a stranger in this world. You're different than the guy next door.

Are Your Prayers Hindered?

Maybe you've heard God stops listening to your prayers too. There's a sin blockage, some claim, so He can't hear them. Some even quote 1 Peter 3:7 out of context to support such a view:

> *Husbands, in the same way be considerate as you live with your wives, and treat them with respect as the weaker partner and as heirs with you of the gracious gift of life, so that nothing will hinder your prayers.* (1 Peter 3:7)

It's obvious that Peter is talking about a husband and wife praying together. If they are fighting with one another, their prayer life *together* will be hindered. In other words, they simply won't pray with each other.

This passage has nothing to do with God not hearing your prayers. Not to mention, just five verses later, Peter says, "the eyes of the Lord are on *the righteous*, and *his ears are attentive to their prayer*" (1 Peter 3:12a). As a child of God, you are "the righteous," and your Father hears your prayers at all times.

God does not turn a deaf ear when you're struggling. Quite the opposite: It's His attentive ear and constant presence that enable you to escape the clutches of temptation.

Bottom Line

When it comes to the finished work of Christ, there's no fly in the ointment. There's no worm in the apple. You're a totally forgiven person. As a result, you're in fellowship with God, twenty-four hours a day, seven days a week, without interruption, now and into eternity. And He always hears your prayers.

God is not in a barbershop chair, swiveling away when you sin. Yes, there are unavoidable consequences to sin. But God's face is always toward you (1 Peter 3:12). He never revokes His presence. And it is His never-ending grace that teaches you to say "no" to sin (Titus 2:11–12; Romans 6:17).

CHAPTER 26

Melinda stumbled upon our radio program as she was flipping through the channels on her SiriusXM radio one night on her way home from work. What I was talking about caught her attention, so she wrote me an email as soon as she got home:

"I didn't grow up in church, but I got saved recently," she said. And then she went on to share a heartbreaking story.

"I was trafficked when I was younger," she explained, "and even now I'm struggling against a compulsion to go back to prostitution. It doesn't help that I feel so unclean. There's no way God could possibly accept someone like me.

"When I was saved, they told me God would accept me. But it just doesn't feel like He does, and I don't know how to get past this. I take communion every Sunday, and I ask for forgiveness for my past. I'm really tired of how I've failed God, but I can't seem to find a way forward. I'm still stuck in the past."

Melinda is not alone in her confusion. The reality is that Christians all over the world don't fully realize their total forgiveness in Christ. They've adopted an apology-driven economy for sins rather than God's blood-driven economy for sins.

But remember, Jesus shed His blood once; it worked the first time, and there's no repeat needed. No amount of apologizing, confessing, or asking for forgiveness will make you more forgiven than you already are.

However, since the Lord's Supper is a regular practice in churches around the world, you can see why people like Melinda might begin to view it as a cleansing ritual. Maybe you've experienced something like this: The bread and wine have been prepared and will soon be served. You've been told you have about ninety seconds to get clean and right with God before the elements come down your aisle. Everyone around you has bowed their heads to pray and ask for forgiveness for the last week or month (or year) of sins. You might even hear some people weeping due to their recent track record.

Now, don't get me wrong: I believe regret over sin is healthy. But should masses of believers be analyzing their recent performance just before the cup hits their row?

No, that was never God's intention!

The Lord's Supper

Wait a minute: Aren't you supposed to examine yourself? Don't you need to confess your sins before you take the Lord's Supper to get back in right standing with God?

This is a common misconception. You're actually told to celebrate the Lord's Supper "in remembrance" of Christ, not in remembrance of your sins (Luke 22:19; 1 Corinthians 11:24). So where did the idea of dimming the lights and examining yourself before partaking really start?

It stems from a gross misinterpretation of this passage:

> *So then, whoever eats the bread or drinks the cup of the Lord in an unworthy manner will be guilty of sinning against the body and blood of the Lord. Everyone ought to **examine themselves before** they eat of the bread and drink from the cup. For those who eat and drink without discerning the body of Christ eat and drink **judgment** on themselves.* (1 Corinthians 11:27–29)

Ouch. Drinking judgment on yourself? Eating in an unworthy manner? Sinning against the body and blood of Jesus? What is this all about? And what do we need to examine? We find our answer as we back up about ten verses in the same passage. Here's what we find:

> *I hear that when you come together as a church, there are **divisions** among you, and to some extent I believe it.* (1 Corinthians 11:18)

Apparently, the Corinthians were bickering about something related to the Lord's Supper. As we read further, we discover some people were showing up early, eating up all the food, and drinking up all the wine.

... for when you are eating, some of you go ahead with **your own private suppers.** *As a result, one person remains* **hungry** *and another gets* **drunk.** *Don't you have homes to eat and drink in? Or do you despise the church of God by* **humiliating those who have nothing?** *What shall I say to you? Shall I praise you? Certainly not in this matter!* (1 Corinthians 11:21–22)

Gluttony. Drunkenness. At the Lord's Supper? This problem couldn't occur today in most churches with our thimble-sized serving of Welch's grape juice and our crouton-sized morsel of bread!

But in the early-church context, the Lord's Supper was celebrated with a full meal. The Corinthians' gluttony and drunkenness humiliated the poor people who would show up to the meal and find nothing left. This is not surprising, given we're talking about Corinth—a city filled with debauchery. Think of Corinth like Las Vegas, then throw in spring break, then add Mardi Gras. That's Corinth.

This was the "unworthy manner" in which they were conducting the Lord's Supper. This is why they needed to examine what they were doing. It was about the inappropriate ways they were celebrating the supper. It was never supposed to be about rummaging through our recent performance to see if we qualify. Nevertheless, two thousand years later, we've convoluted the meaning of the passage. As a result, the Lord's Supper has become a ritual of examination. We're inspecting our sins instead of our Savior. We're looking to our track record instead of His finished work.

Paul just wanted them to be considerate of each other as they celebrated the Lord's Supper. Their parties had gotten so bad that some of them were even getting sick and passing out (or dying!) from alcoholism and gluttony (1 Corinthians 11:30). That's why Paul concludes with the simple solution of waiting for one another. And he says if you're that hungry, eat something at home first.

> So then, my brothers and sisters, when you gather to eat, you should all eat **together**. Anyone who is hungry should **eat something at home**, so that when you meet together it may not result in judgment. (1 Corinthians 11:33–34a)

Judgment? What kind of judgment? Judgment from God? No, here they're gathering, and instead of celebrating in a unified manner, they end up fighting and judging each other for their selfish actions. This is what led to the divisions among them (1 Corinthians 11:18).

This simple reason—gluttony, drunkenness, and divisions at the supper—is why they needed to examine their practices. Yes, in context, "everyone ought to examine themselves" was about Corinthian debauchery during the Lord's Supper. It was never a call for us to dim the lights, play sad music, and get introspective about our recent performance.

The Bottom Line

Do you see the irony in our faulty interpretation of this passage? Here's a supper designed to get us to reflect on Jesus, who qualified us through the cross and the resurrection. And as we participate, we're still trying to get qualified?

The whole point of the Lord's Supper is to celebrate all Jesus did to qualify you. You don't need to qualify for the celebration if Jesus qualified you. Instead, you can raise your glass toward Heaven and confidently toast the finished work of Christ. You can celebrate the Lord's Supper—not in remembrance of your track record, but in remembrance of Him.

He has qualified you! So, next time you celebrate the Lord's Supper, ask yourself: Am I thinking about my sins or my Savior?

> *Let us fix our eyes on Jesus*, *the author and perfecter of our faith, who for the joy set before him endured the cross, scorning its shame, and sat down at the right hand of the throne of God.* (Hebrews 12:2)

CHAPTER 27

Carlos was visiting our church for the first time, sizing us up, and something I'd said during the sermon just didn't add up. So he cornered me after the service to get things straight.

"Did I hear you right?" he asked. "Did you really say we don't have to ask God for forgiveness? Don't you know what it says in the Lord's Prayer? Jesus Himself said we should ask God for forgiveness! What you're teaching makes no sense!"

"Carlos, I understand your hesitation," I said. "I would have questions too if I were in your shoes. But I would ask you to consider this: The Lord's Prayer was offered to Jews in the context of the Sermon on the Mount—before the cross, before the resurrection, before Pentecost, and before the born-again experience we enjoy today. Don't you think the cross changes an issue like our forgiveness?"

"Of course, the cross is our means to forgiveness," Carlos replied, "but we still have to ask for it . . . and Jesus told us to!" he exclaimed.

"Not exactly," I said. "Jesus didn't just say to ask for forgiveness. It was more specific than that. He taught them to ask God to forgive them *to the same degree they had forgiven other people.* In the same sermon, He also taught them to chop off body parts in their fight against sin and to get right with others before going to the altar to make animal sacrifices. There's a context there that's worth considering."

A Conditional Prayer

My conversation with Carlos highlights an important question: How does the Lord's Prayer fit in if we have once-for-all forgiveness? Remember, the idea of asking for forgiveness appears zero times in the New Testament letters. So what's going on with Jesus's prayer?

First, we see Jesus telling His followers not to engage in mindless repetition of prayers. He says God doesn't listen to them because of their many words (Matthew 6:7). It's a bit ironic, then, that two thousand years later, we see people mindlessly memorizing this Matthew 6 prayer and reciting it over and over in church!

In the prayer, we don't merely see an asking for forgiveness. That's not what Jesus is teaching. No, it's more specific than that. Jesus is instructing them to *ask God to forgive them in the same way and to the same degree they've forgiven other people* (Matthew 6:12).

Imagine asking God to give to you the same treatment you've given to others. Now, that's a deathtrap . . . and that's the whole point!

Surely, they've harbored bitterness and resentment against others and haven't forgiven them perfectly. If God were to forgive them only to the same degree they've forgiven others, they could never enter His Kingdom.

The Clear Condition

Still not sure Jesus was presenting conditional forgiveness to expose their bitter hearts? If there's any doubt, Jesus's conclusion at the end of the prayer clears it up.

> For *if you forgive other people* when they sin against you, your heavenly Father **will** also forgive you. But *if you do not forgive others* their sins, your Father **will not** forgive your sins. (Matthew 6:14–15)

Without a doubt, Jesus is setting up a clear condition for those who want to be forgiven by God. If they do their part in forgiving others first, God will do His part and forgive them. If they don't forgive others first, God will not forgive them either. Similarly, in this same sermon, Jesus says they'll be judged by God to the same degree they've judged others (Matthew 7:1–2).

Is this true for believers in Christ today? Does God only forgive us to the same degree we've forgiven others? Does God only forgive the "nice" Christians? Should we then imitate

God and only forgive nice people too? And is God's judgment
of us dependent on our judgment of other people?

Certainly not! We see the polar opposite of this in both
Ephesians 4:32 and Colossians 3:13.

> *Be kind and compassionate to one another,* ***forgiving***
> ***each other****, just as in Christ God* ***forgave*** *you.*
> (Ephesians 4:32)

> *Bear with each other and* ***forgive one another*** *if any of*
> *you has a grievance against someone. Forgive as the*
> *Lord* ***forgave*** *you.* (Colossians 3:13)

Yes, you and I are called to forgive other people—but *not*
to earn God's forgiveness. Instead, we're invited to pass on to
others the same forgiveness God has given us. Which came
first? God's forgiveness of our sins. What comes second? Our
forgiveness of other people.

But this is counter to what we read in the Lord's Prayer.
So how do we reconcile the two? We don't. The Lord's Prayer
is before the cross, before once-for-all forgiveness was given
at Calvary. Meanwhile, Ephesians and Colossians contain
instruction for life under the New Covenant, after the cross.

The Tough Love of Jesus

Galatians 4:4 tells us that Jesus was "born under the law."
And His audience was under the Law. So how do you communicate with people who are living under a system based on

achieving? Do you pat them on the back and tell them they're doing fine when they're nowhere near the true standard?

What we see from Jesus is tough love. He points out His audience's hypocrisy. He shows them if they were to receive from God what they've been dishing out to others, they'd be doomed. Jesus exposes their slavery to bitterness and resentment. He helps them see they don't deserve forgiveness from God. Any forgiveness from Him would have to come by His grace. And that's the whole point.

Remember, the Sermon on the Mount is *a killer sermon*. It reveals the true standard of the Law, the spiritual death of humanity, and the hypocrisy of everyone. The forgiveness taught in the Lord's Prayer is no exception. I'm sure Jesus's listeners could barely finish the prayer itself if they realized what they were saying: "Lord, forgive me in the same way I've forgiven others." That gulp in their throat was the effect Jesus was going for!

You may recall that, in this same sermon, Jesus tells them to pluck out their eye and cut off their hand in their fight against sin (Matthew 5:29–30). He tells them that looking at someone with lust is the same as adultery and anger against someone equals murdering them (Matthew 5:21–22, 27–28). He caps off the sermon by telling His listeners to "be perfect" like God (Matthew 5:48). Clearly, they weren't going to make it out of the sermon alive. Well, the prayer in Matthew 6 carries the same purpose as the rest of the sermon. It exposes everyone as undeserving hypocrites who will never measure up to the Law's true standard and therefore need God's grace more than they ever realized.

The Bottom Line

On this side of the cross, you as a believer can confidently say you're forgiven of all your sins—past, present, and future. You're not forgiven because you forgave other people first. You're forgiven because Christ died for your sins (Romans 5:8). God was the initiator, and you responded.

There's no need for walking on eggshells with your God. He canceled your debt. Now, you forgive others because He already forgave you—completely and forever.

CHAPTER 28

I was recently doing a Zoom event with some families who'd been watching our church services online and wanted to share some issues that had come up. A woman named Jenny asked this:

"I'm in a ladies' Bible study on Wednesday mornings, and right now we're studying the Gospel of John. I feel like I'm in two worlds at once, because I stream your church service online, and I hear we believers are totally forgiven of all our sins. But then I go to this study, and they're saying we need a daily foot-washing like Jesus did for Peter.

"Our Bible study leaders say we're 'clean, but not all' of us, like Jesus said to the disciples, so we need daily confession to get clean," she continued. "I know this doesn't line up with the Gospel. But I don't understand what Jesus meant in John

13, so I want your take on it. It can't mean what they're saying, can it?"

"No, Jenny, it doesn't mean that at all," I said.

Jesus's statement is not birthed out of thin air, I explained. The conversation starts with Peter. Peter is the one who asks for his whole body to be washed. And Jesus basically responds, "That's what a bath is for!"

Then He tells the group they're already clean, except for Judas. So Jesus is washing feet—and only feet—to demonstrate servanthood. We shouldn't be developing a doctrine out of Peter's confused state or his need for a bath! And, again, this is not a theology of forgiveness and cleansing. It's simply a demonstration of serving one another in love.

Today's Foot-Washing Fetish

I've been asked Jenny's question hundreds of times over the last few decades. Even though the finished work of the cross is clear in Scripture, many are still looking for any reason to play a part in their own forgiveness. Hence, they interpret the John 13 conversation between Peter and Jesus to be about "spiritual foot-washing" to get daily forgiveness from God.

But Jesus is simply offering an example of radical servanthood:

> *Now that I, your Lord and Teacher, have washed your feet, **you also should wash one another's feet. I have set you an example** that you should do as I have done for you.* (John 13:14–15)

He's demonstrating what it means to serve one another. His instruction was never about getting more forgiveness each day.

Jesus only washed Peter's feet *once*, and He certainly didn't bathe Peter that morning! The idea that we need daily touch-ups from Christ is not the point of the passage. Foot-washing was a custom of the day. When Jesus washed the feet of His disciples, it was a demonstration of humble service.

It was never about needing more forgiveness.

But what about in verse 10, when Jesus says, "You are clean, but not all of you"? Doesn't that mean that—spiritually—only *part* of you is forgiven and you need more cleansing each day? As I explained to Jenny, Jesus was referring to Judas! The next verse says, "for he knew who was going to betray him."

Clearly, this passage is about serving the disciples. And it's about identifying Judas as a traitor. There's no place here for concocting a foot-washing-for-forgiveness theology. That's an insult to the finished work of Christ!

Blasphemy against the Holy Spirit

We had just finished four sessions of our conference in Dallas. Conner raised his hand during the Q&A and said, "I'd like for you to explain the one thing that will not be forgiven—blasphemy against the Holy Spirit. If we're totally forgiven, then how can there be one that's not forgiven?"

This was my answer to Conner:

"Great question, Conner. Matthew 12 presents us with one sin that'll never be forgiven: blasphemy against God's

Spirit. How can it be that there's one sin that won't be forgiven if Jesus died to take away all our sins?

"Here, blasphemy means not believing in the identity and work of Jesus. They thought Jesus was of the devil. Blasphemy against the Spirit was refusing to believe Jesus is the Son of God and refusing to believe His miracles were of God. In short, this blasphemy is rejecting the person and work of Christ.

"Today, it takes the form of rejecting the Gospel itself, since the Gospel centers on the person and work of Christ. And it comes as no surprise that a person is not forgiven for rejecting the Gospel. They are left without a Savior, so they remain in an unforgiven state. They are still dead in their sins.

"It makes sense, right? If we reject life, we remain dead. We have to believe Jesus has the power to save us in order to call upon Him in the first place. Simply put, there's no forgiveness in Adam. Forgiveness is ours only when we believe in Jesus."

The Bottom Line

Blasphemy against the Spirit is unforgivable. Why? Because you're rejecting the Spirit. If you reject the Spirit of Grace, how do you expect to find grace? If you reject the Spirit, how do you expect to be born of Him? If you reject Jesus, how do you expect to find forgiveness? There's no forgiveness outside of Him. There's no eternal life elsewhere, either.

Believers don't have to worry about blasphemy against the Spirit. We can't commit this blasphemy. It's impossible for us to commit it. We've already believed in the person and work of Jesus Christ. We've already received total forgiveness and new life in Him.

> For by one offering He has **perfected for all time** those who are sanctified. (Hebrews 10:14 NASB)

> And that is what some of you were. But you **were washed**, you **were sanctified**, you **were justified** in the name of the Lord Jesus Christ and by the Spirit of our God. (1 Corinthians 6:11)

CHAPTER 29

Gary had been a Christian most of his life, but he wasn't experiencing any joy in his life. In fact, things seemed to be getting worse over time.

"I feel like I'm constantly overwhelmed by the Holy Spirit's conviction. As I become more aware of all the sin in my life, I just get discouraged," he shared.

"What kind of sins are we talking about here, Gary?" I asked.

"Well, just everything. A lustful thought, a selfish thought, so many things hit me throughout the day. And here's the thing. I know it doesn't have to be this way," he said despondently. "There's a woman in our office who's a Christian, too. But every time I see her, she is overflowing with joy. She focuses on grace, and I seem to only focus on my sins. Yet we both believe the same thing, don't we? I want to be more like her, but I just don't know how."

"Have you thought about focusing more on grace yourself?" I asked.

"I would like to, but how can I when the Spirit is constantly convicting me?" Gary responded.

"Gary, what if I told you that's not the Holy Spirit convicting you?" I asked.

"Not the Holy Spirit?" Gary looked surprised.

"Yes, you heard me," I said. "It's not the Holy Spirit. First, it's not a sin to simply receive a sinful thought. But more importantly, the Holy Spirit doesn't hound you about your performance to the point that you're so distracted you can't even think about God's grace."

"Are you saying it's Satan?" Gary asked.

"Gary, do you see that in thirty seconds of me questioning the messages you're getting, your new best guess is that it's Satan, not God?" I replied. "This should tell you something. The Bible literally says the enemy accuses us day and night, and his goal is to steal our joy and kill our contentment. I'd say that what you're experiencing is condemnation, not conviction of the Spirit."

"But doesn't God care about my behavior?" Gary asked, confused.

"Yes, of course He cares about your behavior," I said, "But He brings about change in your life by convincing you of your new heart and your new desires, not by convicting you as if you're a felon awaiting sentencing."

"So how can I recognize the difference between the two?" Gary asked—still puzzled but looking a bit more hopeful now.

"The Holy Spirit keeps no record of your wrongs. He remembers your sins no more," I said. "When you're so beat up and distracted by your sin record that you can hardly function, you need to know that's not God. He doesn't operate that way."

"Okay, I see what you're saying, but give me an example. If I'm lusting after someone, how does the Spirit react?" Gary asked. He was starting to get it, but he wanted a practical example.

"The Holy Spirit bears witness with your spirit about who you really are," I explained. "He's your Comforter and Counselor in that situation. He says, 'Gary, you're better than that thought. That lustful thought is beneath you, and you're above it, raised and seated with Me. That'll never make you fulfilled. You're dead to that thought and alive to Me. You're made for so much more, so fix your eyes on Me, and enjoy true satisfaction.'"

"If that's the Spirit," Gary said, "then I've been way off in what I've been listening to!"

"Exactly," I said. "Now, you can believe the truth about yourself and fix your eyes on Jesus, undistracted by the accusations of the enemy. This will do more for your attitudes and actions than any of this morbid introspection has ever done."

Conviction of the Holy Spirit

What does total forgiveness in Christ mean for the conviction of the Holy Spirit? After all, God remembers your sins no more. And Hebrews 10:17 says the Holy Spirit Himself doesn't remember your sins. So why would He be "convicting" you of something He doesn't remember? Why would He be "convicting" you of something He keeps no record of and never holds against you?

Simple. He wouldn't.

The truth is the word "convict" is never used to express how the Holy Spirit relates to a believer. We humans typically use the word "convict" for a convict, someone who was on trial and was convicted. Next, they await punishment. This does not describe how the Holy Spirit relates to us as children of God. No, the idea of "conviction" is reserved exclusively for the Spirit's work in the lives of unbelievers:

> *And He, when He comes, will convict **the world** regarding sin, and righteousness, and judgment: regarding sin, **because they do not believe in Me**. (John 16:8–9 NASB)*

The Holy Spirit convicts the world, because it does not believe in Jesus. So if the Holy Spirit is not "convicting" believers, then how does He relate to you?

The Holy Spirit is your Counselor, Comforter, and Guide into all truth (John 16:13). He never treats you as a convict. He simply bears witness to your true calling as God's child (Romans 8:16).

Yes, He's concerned about your behavior and how you treat others. But His method is different from anything you've experienced before. He's training you for the future, not punishing you for the past. *He reminds you that you're above sin, sin is beneath you, and you're not made for sin.* He's not "convicting" you of your sins. He's convincing you of your righteousness!

Stop the Double-Talk!

We've got to stop all the double-talk about our forgiveness. Father and Son and Holy Spirit agree that our sins are gone. This has a direct impact on how God treats us when we fail. God never guilts us or shames us into changing our behavior. Instead, His Spirit inspires us from within by pointing us to our new heart and our new identity in Him.

Let's come to grips with the plain, straightforward truth that we believers are totally forgiven people, no matter what. *To believe anything less is to equate the blood of Jesus with the blood of animals shed in the Old Testament.*

Let's begin shouting from the rooftops that we have the best thing going. We have something better than any world religion. We have total forgiveness, complete cleansing, and perfect standing before God, all the time. Such incredible grace is only found in Jesus, and we can brag on His name!

*I am writing to you, dear children, because **your sins have been forgiven on account of his name**.* (1 John 2:12)

CHAPTER 30

Ken called in to a live radio interview I was doing one afternoon. He said, "I like what you say, and I listen to you a lot, Andrew. But I'm concerned about some of the things you teach."

"Which things?" I asked. (There's a lot to choose from!)

"There are people in my life who say they're believers," Ken said, "but they continue to choose sin, whether it's fornicating or coveting their neighbor's belongings. When you say they're forgiven, it seems to me that kind of grace leads to more of that same sinful lifestyle, because there are no consequences for their sin."

Ken's question isn't a new one. New Testament believers asked Paul about this too, so I knew what to say. "Ken, you're expressing an age-old concern here," I replied. "You want the answer to a very important question: Does the teaching of

God's forgiveness lead to more sinning or less sinning? Do struggling believers need more grace or less grace? Maybe they need the forgiveness withheld? Maybe they need some Law? That's ultimately your question, and we can only get our answer from Scripture—not from our intuition or opinion."

Titus tells us the grace of God teaches us to say "no" to sin (Titus 2:11–12). Peter writes that if we lack godly qualities in our behavior, it is because we've forgotten our forgiveness (2 Peter 1:9). Apparently, the solution for us believers who sin is to remember who we are and more fully celebrate our forgiveness. Struggling believers always need more grace, not less.

I wanted to make this real for Ken, so I said, "Let's think specifically of one of these people you are referring to: someone you think is a true believer but is stuck in a pattern of sin. Now, let's ask: Which of these two options do you think will work better?"

Then I shared these scenarios with Ken:

Option 1: You show up on their doorstep and you say, "Here are ten laws that I would like to tell you about: 'Thou shalt not steal. Thou shalt not commit adultery. Thou shalt not covet.' And you continue reading through these laws and deliver them with a final comment, 'These are important. So please stop sinning, and you're not forgiven until you do stop.'"

Option 2: You show up on their doorstep and say, "Hey, I know you're struggling. I know you've got to be torn up inside, but you know what? You're not made for that. You're above sin. Sin is beneath you, and you're better than sin. You're forgiven. God looks at you as if you've never sinned a day in your life. You are spotless and blameless, and God thinks the world of you. He's given you a new heart. He's given you a new spirit. He's put His Spirit inside of you and motivates you by His grace.

"I'm not here to point a bony finger of judgment at you. Instead, I want to share God's grace with you: Do you know He's crazy about you? Do you know that He dances over you and delights in you? He's not holding any of your sins against you. He's made you clean and close, and He's going to inspire you and grow you up in Him.

"So be ready for His counsel, as He's going to lead you to a place of true contentment through new perspectives and choices. He loves you!"

Which Message?

"Which of these two messages do you believe is more effective?" I asked Ken. "Is it the 'You've got to stop sinning, or else' message? Does withholding the truth about the finished work of Christ work best? Or should we go with what the Bible teaches? It says sin won't master them under God's grace. Apart from the Law, sin is dead. God's grace teaches them to say 'no' to sin.

"This second message is the one that actually works," I continued. "I've seen it time and again. It's the message the church so desperately needs to hear."

People say this total-forgiveness message is a license to sin. To that, I always say: "You were sinning just fine without a license! So, what if you trusted God's grace for a change?" Jesus said, "It is finished." Evidently, He knew what He was doing. He forgave you once for all. That's a really big motivator, and you need to know it.

Is Total Forgiveness Dangerous?

People get nervous about the message of total forgiveness. Is it dangerous? Will it lead to more sinning? Jesus told us a person who is forgiven much loves much (Luke 7:47). What if that's actually true?

It is true.

As I shared with Ken, Peter tells us if we lack godly qualities in our lives, it's simply because we've forgotten our purification. What we need is more grace, not less grace. We really can trust God's grace to teach us to say "no" to sin:

> For **the grace of God** has appeared, bringing salvation to all people, **instructing us to deny ungodliness** and worldly desires **and to live sensibly**, righteously, and in a godly manner in the present age. (Titus 2:11–12)

Am I saying you should just ignore the issue of sin? Do you just keep right on sinning?

Of course not! I'm not saying that at all. I'm simply saying you're as forgiven today as you'll ever be. After all, here's what it would take for you to be more forgiven: Jesus would have to come to Earth and hang on a cross all over again. But He's never going to do that because the cross worked the first time.

Yes, you turn from sin, and you say "no" to sin, every single time. There are plenty of reasons to consider your wrongdoing and turn away from it. But you don't need more forgiveness. You turn from sin to get more fulfilled but not more forgiven.

Let me be clear: A Christian can be totally forgiven yet miserable. God doesn't want that for you. He wants you to experience His best.

The longing of your heart after you've sinned is not to get more forgiveness and cleansing. You already have those. The longing of your heart is to turn from sin and experience all you're intended for. God wants to train you for the future, not punish you for the past. He's coaching you for the days ahead without keeping any record of your wrongs. That's the truth of what you're experiencing after a sin struggle. It is the tugging of God's Spirit to remind you you're forgiven and to tell you you're made for so much more.

Sin is beneath you. You're above it. After all, you're raised and seated with Christ!

The Bottom Line

I understand the panic people experience when they first hear the Hebrews 10:14 message of complete forgiveness—past, present, and future. Many times, their reaction is: "Are you saying I can just go out and do whatever I want?"

To that I respond, "Are you saying you want to sin?"

The Bible says otherwise. Apparently, God is not afraid of what you want. He says you're a slave of righteousness. You can't get away from it. You can't help but crave it. You want what God wants. Nothing else will fulfill you.

It seems that God can afford to forgive your next sin ahead of time. He knows that when you commit it, you won't be content anyway. You will want change. The longing for something better is hardwired within you. God knows that. He put it there!

The solution is never to water down the blood of Jesus or to hedge concerning your total forgiveness in Christ. No, you should be adamant about what the blood of Jesus accomplished for you. You can also be excited about the new, obedient heart God gave you. Both are essential elements of the Gospel. If you leave one out, the message makes no sense (and then it's no wonder people object to it).

God could afford to totally forgive you because He also made you new at the core. He knew exactly what He was doing. The Gospel is the most intelligent and beautiful message on the planet.

PART 4

GOD IS AN EQUAL-OPPORTUNITY EMPLOYER

CHAPTER 31

"I messed up my marriage so bad," Carol said. "I made so many mistakes, and it's all my fault. I had such a good thing going, and I ruined it. Now, I'm stuck. I'll never be able to make up for this."

I'd just finished a sermon at a church I was visiting in California. Carol had come up to me afterward to see if I could offer her any hope with something that had clearly been eating at her for a long time.

"What exactly happened?" I asked.

"I wish I could go back and do it all over again and do it right," Carol said, "But now he's already with someone else, and I'm in a new marriage too. My mind plays tricks on me, because I know I can't go back in time, but I also don't feel right or settled in my new relationship. I even heard a Bible teacher on the radio say that, because I've had a divorce and I'm now remarried, I'm a perpetual adulterer!"

"A perpetual adulterer?" I asked. "Well, the only 'perpetual' thing you are is a perpetual child of God. You're not an adulterer. God doesn't see you that way at all, Carol, and you need to know that. I don't know everything that you heard, but the truth will always set you free."

Carol didn't think I understood her the first time, so she explained again. "What he was saying on the radio was that, because I had ruined my first marriage and it resulted in divorce, getting remarried was a sin. Therefore, as long as I remain in my new marriage, I am sinning and will be judged by God for it. That doesn't exactly make for a great marriage!"

"I hear you. It certainly doesn't," I affirmed. "You can't wake up every day and continue to build a healthy marriage if you think it's sinful and that you'll face judgment for it! But fortunately, that's just not the truth. No matter what happened in your past, you're forgiven, and you're living in the present with God today. He looks at you as if you've never sinned a day in your life. He wants you to be able to focus on today and not rewind to the past. His total forgiveness allows you to do so."

"So, I'm not living in sin by staying married to my husband?" Carol asked, hope dawning.

"No," I said. "Two wrongs don't make a right. For you to divorce your current husband to try to go back to your previous husband—who is now remarried and won't take you anyway—makes no sense. God wants you to live in the present, to know that any sins of the past are fully forgiven, and to give thanks for your current husband who loves you. As far as the Final Judgment goes, you're as safe as Jesus Himself. You'll never be judged for your failures. Christ took away all your sins through the cross."

Carol looked relieved to hear what I had to say. For the first time, she had a sense that her current marriage could continue and even flourish under God's grace.

Do the Math and Celebrate!

Some people say they agree their sins are forgiven, taken away, and remembered no more. But then, they also believe they'll answer for their sins at the Final Judgment.

Do they not see the contradiction? How could we answer for our sins when the only just answer would be that we deserve death?

Remember: The "wages of sin is death." Jesus died and took the wages. There are no wages left. So let's do the math and celebrate. We don't owe God!

You won't be judged for your sins. You were already judged for them, and the verdict was guilty. The punishment was death. That's why Jesus died on your behalf. And Hebrews 9 says Jesus is coming back for you—not to judge your sins, but to bring you salvation.

> . . . *so Christ also, having been offered once to bear the sins of many, will appear a second time* **for salvation without reference to sin**, *to those who* **eagerly** *await Him.* (Hebrews 9:28 NASB)

The Day of Judgment: Revelation

Even when you realize your sins are not taken into account, events at the Final Judgment can still be confusing. But it doesn't have to be that way. The issue of judgment doesn't need to remain unclear. If God says He remembers your sins no more *now*, will He remember them later?

No.

In Revelation 20, a group called "the dead" are pulled up from Hell and judged. Their names are not found in the Book of Life, and they're judged according to their deeds. They're unbelievers. The verdict is guilty, and they're thrown into the Lake of Fire.

Then chapter 21 begins, and the Church appears on the scene. The Bride of Christ is invited into an eternity that involves no pain and no sorrow.

It's essential that we identify which group we belong to: the one judged in chapter 20 or the one celebrating in chapter 21. Jesus helps us understand our place when He says, "the one who believes in Him is not judged" (John 3:18 NASB).

The Day of Judgment: Matthew

Matthew 25 also presents a picture of the Final Judgment that involves two groups: sheep and goats.

> *When the Son of Man comes in his glory, and all the angels with him, he will sit on his glorious throne. All the nations will be gathered before him, and he will separate the people one from another as a shepherd separates the*

sheep from the goats. *He will put the sheep on his right and the goats on his left*. (Matthew 25:31–33)

Jesus then says the sheep will be given an inheritance and be invited into the kingdom prepared for them (verse 34). Conversely, the goats are told, "Depart from me, you who are cursed, into the eternal fire prepared for the devil and his angels" (verse 41). Notice the two different groups and the two different outcomes.

At this Final Judgment, there are only sheep and goats. There are no shoats, and there are no geep. There's no hybrid animal or gray area. Verse 46 summarizes the outcome clearly: The goats go away to punishment, and the righteous enjoy eternal life. So if you're a sheep, you have nothing to worry about!

The Bottom Line

Clearly, we have nothing to fear at the Day of Judgment. The Apostle John tells us that God's perfect love casts out our fear. Any fear we might feel is because we imagine punishment, but there is no punishment (1 John 4:18).

The simple truth is that we'll never be judged for our sins. God has obliterated our sin record forever (Romans 4:8; Hebrews 8:12).

CHAPTER 32

When I was a teenager, my youth pastor figured out when Jesus was coming back, and it was soon. Yes, seriously. He'd been doing some research. Once he'd decided Christ's return was less than twenty-four hours away, he gathered the youth group together for a special meeting so we could prepare.

"Jesus is coming back tomorrow," he said, "so you'd better get right with the Lord now, before it's too late."

Everybody was freaking out. There was crying and panic attacks. Some people were on their knees listing every sin they could remember and begging God to forgive them. Others were just plain scared. I didn't know what to do; my mom had pulled me aside before I went to the meeting and told me it wasn't true. But what if she was wrong?

You'd think believers would be excited if they knew Jesus was coming back, but no one in our youth group was! Why not? Because they were imagining the big movie screen in the sky displaying all their sins at the Final Judgment.

But here's the great news: There's no movie. God destroyed the reel!

First John 4 says we can have confidence on the Day of Judgment because we are like Jesus (1 John 4:17). This means we're as safe and secure at the Final Judgment as Jesus Himself. If we're fearing the Final Judgment, John says it's because we're imagining punishment when there is none for us. We can simply rest in God's perfect love:

> *This is how love is made complete among us so that we will have **confidence on the day of judgment:** In this world we are **like Jesus**. There is no fear in love. But perfect love drives out fear, because **fear has to do with punishment**. The one who fears is not **made perfect in love**.* (1 John 4:17–18)

Recognize that God's love, by definition, keeps no record of wrongs (1 Corinthians 13:5). Over time, as you set your mind on God's love for you, any fear of judgment will be driven out and replaced with an unshakeable confidence. That's God's agenda for you—to establish you and strengthen you in His perfect love.

A Gospel Building

What about 1 Corinthians 3? This passage is often used to justify a final judgment of believers' sins:

*For no one can lay any foundation other than the one already laid, which is Jesus Christ. If anyone builds on this foundation using gold, silver, costly stones, wood, hay, or straw, their work will be shown for what it is, because the Day will bring it to light. It will be revealed with fire, and **the fire will test the quality of each person's work**.* (1 Corinthians 3:11–13)

When you're building a house, it's important to get the foundation right. But even if you get it right, the workmanship that follows is also important. You don't want low-quality materials or poor workmanship on top of a good foundation.

That's what is in focus here: *the foundation of the Gospel message and what comes next*. Paul laid a proper foundation, and he wanted quality materials to be used for the rest of the building. Paul—a master builder—taught the Corinthians the essentials of the faith. Apollos came along after Paul to build on that foundation. Paul's point is that if any other communicators show up later and teach a different gospel, then it's no gospel at all. It will not stand the test of time, and the final judgment will reveal it for what it truly is: a message built of wood, hay, and stubble.

This passage is about the message itself and the messenger's work. A messenger will suffer loss of his work, with nothing to show for it, if it's not built on Jesus. It has nothing to do with believers being judged for their sins!

"Depart from Me!"

Maybe you've also wondered about this well-known passage in which Jesus rejects a group of people at the Final Judgment:

*Many will say to me on that day, "Lord, Lord, did we not **prophesy** in your name and in your name **drive out** demons and in your name **perform** many miracles?" Then I will tell them plainly, "**I never knew you. Away from me, you evildoers!**"* (Matthew 7:22–23)

We just read Paul's warning to the Corinthians about false teachers' building on a good foundation. Here in Matthew 7, Jesus issues a similar warning. There are wolves in sheep's clothing. They appear as religious zealots but know nothing of the true Gospel. Their focus is entirely on what they supposedly did rather than what Jesus did for them. They've got a works-based gospel and therefore have missed the real thing. Here again, these are not true believers, so there's nothing to fear. Rest assured: If you're in Christ, you can have total confidence on that glorious day (1 John 4:17).

The Bema Seat of Christ

Second Corinthians 5 has also been used to justify the idea that believers will have to answer for their sins. The passage says:

> **For we must all appear before the judgment seat of Christ,** *so that each of us may* **receive what is due us** *for the things done while in the body,* **whether good or bad.** (2 Corinthians 5:10)

Despite the phrase "we must *all* appear," it's commonly taught that only believers appear at this judgment seat of

Christ. In fact, it's often considered to be a second and separate judgment. I've even heard this "*bema* seat judgment" taught as being a separate event, much like the Olympics. Some claim it's the giving of rewards only (to Christians), and there's no punishment.

But a basic examination of the passage reveals people are recompensed for their *bad* deeds too, not just their good deeds. Furthermore, the word *bema* is used elsewhere in the New Testament to indicate a place of punishment, not just reward. For example, the proconsul Gallio doles out punishment from a *bema* seat (Acts 18:12–17). Clearly, this *bema* seat judgment in 2 Corinthians 5 is not just a sweet event of reward only. Such an idea is nothing but a fabrication!

This judgment event doesn't appear to be any different from the ones we've already seen in Revelation and Matthew. In Revelation, we saw "the dead" versus the Church and two different outcomes at the Great White Throne. In Matthew, we saw the goats and the sheep and two different outcomes. Here, we see *all* of humanity appearing at this *bema* seat and two different outcomes. One group (unbelievers) is recompensed (paid back) for their evil deeds, while another group (believers) is recompensed for their good deeds.

Think about it: Evil deeds are also known as sins. If we believers were recompensed for our sins, it would be death we'd receive. (There is no lesser recompense!) Furthermore, unbelievers cannot be recompensed for their good deeds. They don't have any! Their righteousness is like filthy rags (Isaiah 64:6).

What if the *bema* seat of Christ is a great, white throne? Wouldn't it make sense that God can carry out all of His judgment in one event? Second Corinthians 5:10 is *not* about a second and separate judgment. It's simply a description of the one and only judgment described in Revelation and Matthew.

The Bottom Line

There's one black-and-white judgment, with no gray area, and you'll pass with flying colors. Hebrews 9:28 says Jesus will return to save you "without reference to sin," so you can eagerly await Him. How can you eagerly await Him if you think He's going to bring up all your sins?

You can't.

But the truth is that He'll make no mention of your sins upon His return. Why not? Because He remembers them no more!

CHAPTER 33

Ana called in to our radio program from Colorado with a question. "I heard a preacher on the radio a few weeks ago saying there would be regrets for believers in Heaven," she said.

She went on to explain: "He said the Bible teaches we're not all going to be rewarded the same, and therefore some of us are going to have regrets." Then it got personal. "I already have this legalistic Christian background that I'm trying to shake, and I thought: How in the world can that be true? It just rattles all of the performance anxiety that I'm trying to let go of."

"No wonder it rattled you, Ana," I said. "That's what lies will do to you. Lies will rattle you, and disturb you, and rob you of your peace. Jesus said He came to give you rest in Him.

He said His yoke is easy, and His burden is light, and you would find rest for your soul."

I continued, "It sounds like you're getting a little dose of 'Jesus is fantastic for salvation, but you should be scared out of your wits that you're going to be disappointed in Heaven.' You may not get enough loot. Your mansion may not be big enough. Your jewelry may not be enough to satisfy. You may not get enough crowns or square footage in your mansion. You may be looking around with envy at all the 'better' Christians who got more."

The Truth about Reward(s)

Even though we believers aren't being judged for our sins, shouldn't we expect to receive rewards based on the quantity of our good works? The image some of us have in our minds is that God will increase the square footage in our mansions, or we may get more crowns to stack on our heads, or more jewelry to hang around our necks.

Is this what the Bible really teaches?

We don't see the word "rewards" (plural) in any New Testament letter. Instead, we see there's a reward (singular) for all believers.

In the Parable of the Vineyard Workers (Matthew 20), the landowner hires people to work in his field. He announces he'll give each worker one denarius. Then, after three hours, he hires more workers. At the sixth and ninth hour, he hires more workers. Finally, at the eleventh hour, he hires even more workers.

Hilariously, those who'd been working the least hours jumped in line to receive their paychecks first. They were paid one denarius, as promised. Those further back in the line who'd worked much longer probably thought, "We're really going to score!"

But they all got paid the same.

Then the workers cried out, "This isn't fair. We've been working all day!" But the landowner responded, "Don't I have the right to do what I want with my own money?" (verse 15). Apparently, God is an equal-opportunity employer, and His grace does not stop at the gates of Heaven.

Knowing Christ

If we all get paid the same, what might that "reward" look like?

Paul tells us everything else is garbage next to knowing Christ (Philippians 3:8). What if knowing Jesus is our great reward? And what if that reward begins right now?

> What is more, **I consider everything a loss because of the surpassing worth of knowing Christ Jesus my Lord**, for whose sake I have lost all things. I consider them garbage, that I may gain Christ and be found in him, not having a righteousness of my own that comes from the law, but that which is through faith in Christ—the righteousness that comes from God on the basis of faith. (Philippians 3:8–9)

What else compares to knowing Christ? Nothing. So how is it we believe God is going to be doling out "rewards" unrelated to knowing Him?

The Reward of the Inheritance

There's a reason the word "reward" appears in the singular in the New Testament. The reward we receive is our inheritance as children of God.

> *Whatever you do, work at it with all your heart, as working for the Lord, not for human masters, since you know that **you will receive an inheritance from the Lord as a reward**. It is the Lord Christ you are serving.* (Colossians 3:23–24)

"You'll receive an inheritance from the Lord as a reward." Can it get any more obvious? Our reward is our inheritance. Our inheritance is our reward.

People are always talking about collecting rewards in Heaven. However, they never seem to think *the inheritance* differs from person to person. Here, we see our inheritance and our reward are one and the same.

Furthermore, Peter announces our inheritance is "imperishable" and "undefiled" and "will not fade away" because it is "reserved in heaven" for us (1 Peter 1:4–5). Apparently, we don't have to worry about anything happening to our inheritance or our reward.

Crowns

What about crowns? Doesn't the Bible mention that believers will receive crowns in Heaven?

Yes—in Revelation, John's vision depicts twenty-four elders who have crowns. They toss them like frisbees at Jesus's feet, declaring it's all about Him.

> ... *the twenty-four elders will fall down before Him who sits on the throne, and will worship Him who lives forever and ever, and **will cast their crowns before the throne**, saying, "Worthy are You, our Lord and our God, to receive glory and honor and power...."* (Revelation 4:10–11a)

We see crowns elsewhere in the New Testament. Peter mentions the crown of glory (1 Peter 5:4). Paul talks about the crown of righteousness (2 Timothy 4:8). James refers to the crown of life (James 1:12). Who is our glory if not the Lord? Who is our righteousness if not Jesus? Who is our life if not Christ?

These mentions of the crown of glory, the crown of righteousness, and the crown of life refer to our new life in Jesus, now and into eternity.

He is our glory. He is our righteousness. He is our life.

Store Up Treasures?

We're not collecting certificates redeemable in Heaven's Gift Shop. So what did Jesus mean by "store up for yourselves treasures in Heaven"?

> *But store up for yourselves treasures in heaven, where moths and vermin do not destroy, and where thieves do*

not break in and steal. For where your treasure is, there your heart will be also. (Matthew 6:20–21)

Remember, a treasure is *not* a reward. Treasures are discovered, not earned.

Jesus was challenging His listeners to take on *a heavenly perspective* rather than an earthly one. He was calling them to focus on that which endures the test of time and will be celebrated in eternity. Now remember, they couldn't really rise to the occasion and gain that perspective without the Spirit. However, we can today, since we have the mind of Christ (1 Corinthians 2:16).

CHAPTER 34

"For a decade, my business was booming," Steve wrote in an email to me, "and we experienced significant growth year after year. I was so thankful to God. I was giving out of my excess and feeling blessed to do so.

"But in the last three years," he explained, "things have taken a turn in my life and in my business. Recently, we lost our son. That was devastating, and because of that my marriage has become increasingly strained. We are in counseling, and on top of it all now my business is suffering. I guess I just wonder if I brought this on or what God may be trying to tell me."

Reading between the lines, Steve wondered if the circumstances he was experiencing were his fault. Perhaps God was trying to get his attention. Was God even punishing him for something he'd done?

We've all done it. We've tried to connect the dots between our present circumstances and our past sins. We've looked to our circumstances to decipher what God is trying to "tell" us. Now, there are obvious earthly consequences to some of our choices. But we need to be really careful about "reading the tea leaves" to see what God thinks of us: *Have I fallen out of God's will? Is God mad at me? Is He getting me back for what I did?*

It's tempting to think this way and to lose sight of the truth that God is never angry with you (Romans 5:9). You may easily forget there's no condemnation or punishment from God for your sins. But reality still stands: God is always on your side and in your corner. While Planet Earth comes at you with all kinds of trouble, God is not the author of that trouble. He is not hurling disaster at you to teach you a lesson. Jesus's death on the cross was the full punishment for your sins, so you can let go of the concept of "Christian karma" from God: God is not out to get you!

You can taste and see that the Lord is good (Psalm 34:8). When bad things happen, it doesn't mean God has deserted you. It means you live in a fallen world. When bad things happen, it doesn't mean God doesn't care for you. It simply means God is good and the world is *not*. In those moments, you can recognize God as your Counselor in times of trouble. He's not the cause of the trouble.

Planet Earth comes at you. Christ works in you. Big difference!

Ananias and Sapphira

In Acts 5, a married couple named Ananias and Sapphira lie about how much they donated to the church. Next thing you know, they're dead.

Maybe you've heard if you sin against God, He may take you out like Ananias and Sapphira. Interestingly, though, the passage never says God killed them. It only says they "fell down" and "died." To go any further is to read something into the text that's not really there.

A recent news story told of a pastor on the East Coast who fell down and died of a heart attack at a church meeting when his adultery was discovered. It's possible that Ananias and Sapphira suffered the same fate upon being discovered in their lie. We simply can't know, one way or the other.

But more importantly, we should note the Bible never says they were believers. In fact, it says Satan filled their hearts, which is good evidence they were not believers. Satan can't fill the heart of a believer. We have new, obedient hearts (Romans 6:17), we are sealed by God's Spirit (Ephesians 4:30), and the evil one cannot touch us (1 John 5:18).

Acts is a history book, not a doctrinal book. In Acts, tongues of fire fell on those first believers. That's a historical fact, not a doctrine. In other words, we shouldn't conclude that, without tongues of fire falling on us, we're not genuinely saved. It happened once in the book of Acts, and that makes it history, not doctrine. In the same way, the fact that a married couple fell dead one time in the book of Acts doesn't mean we fashion a doctrine that says God will kill you if you tell a lie. If that were true, church buildings everywhere would be filled with dead bodies!

The Consequences of Sin

According to the law of gravity, what goes up must come down. However, we look up and see objects traveling across the sky: birds, insects, airplanes. To the naked eye, they appear to supersede the law of gravity, at least for a time.

The Bible speaks of the law of sin and death (Romans 8:1–2), which is quite simple: Sin deserves death. But we see a second law that supersedes or overrides the law of sin and death:

> ... *because through Christ Jesus* **the law of the Spirit who gives life** *has set you free from* **the law of sin and death**. (Romans 8:2)

This second law has freed us from the first. You're not under the law of sin and death anymore. When you commit a sin, you don't receive the punishment you deserve.

As we've discussed, you may quench (fail to express) or grieve (deeply concern) God's Spirit when you choose sin (Ephesians 4:30; 1 Thessalonians 5:19). And yes, there are earthly consequences (Galatians 6:8). You drive too fast, and you get a speeding ticket. You eat poorly, and you end up with high cholesterol. You act cruelly to your spouse, and your marriage struggles. There are earthly consequences to your actions. But thank God you never receive the spiritual consequence of sin: death.

The law of the Spirit of life has set you free from the law of sin and death.

God's Loving Discipline

We believers are not punished by God, but what about God's discipline?

In Hebrews 12, we see a description of God's loving discipline. However, the word "scourges" appears in some translations and can really throw people off. Now, if you don't know what scourging is, check out Mel Gibson's film *The Passion of the Christ*. You'll see scourging in vivid detail.

Scourging was not fatherly discipline of a child. It was what Roman soldiers inflicted as punishment upon prisoners, including Jesus. They used an instrument composed of long leather straps and pieces of sharp metal at the end to beat the prisoner. The metal would gouge deeply into the prisoner's back, ripping away skin and muscle, severely injuring or even killing him.

So does God "scourge" His children as discipline?

Here's the truth about this challenging passage: First, the verse includes a quote from the Old Testament, and the bit about scourging doesn't even appear in the original verse (Proverbs 3:12). Also, the Hebrew term *biqqoret* has a double meaning. It can be translated as "scourge" or as "inquire into." Interestingly, the "inquire" meaning is actually older than the "scourge" meaning, as the scourging instrument was invented much later.

Clement (150 to 215 AD) and other scholars thought the epistle to the Hebrews was originally written in Hebrew (which would make sense). The letter mirrors Hebrew poetry in some ways, and there are about 150 words in the epistle that aren't found anywhere else in the New Testament.

This would mean a scribe translating the text to Greek chose to translate *biqqoret* as "scourge" instead of "inquire into." However, given the finished work of the cross and the fact that Jesus took all the punishment for us, the "inquire into" interpretation makes a lot more sense. After all, scourging was punishment, not discipline. Jesus took our punishment in full.

> *But He was wounded for our transgressions, He was bruised for our iniquities; the chastisement for our peace was upon Him, **And by His stripes we are healed**.* (Isaiah 53:5 NKJV)

Jesus was even scourged so we would never be. By His stripes (not ours!), we are healed. God does *deeply inquire* into our lives, because we are His children. He cares for us and wants us to experience His best—Jesus. God disciplines us in loving ways to mold us and shape us and help us think and act in new ways. But He doesn't scourge us!

The Bottom Line

Ephesians 6:4 says not to exasperate our children but instead to bring them up in the training and instruction of the Lord. This tells us God's training and instruction do not exasperate you. He invests in you for your good, so you may share in His holiness (Hebrews 12:10).

You're not a sinner in the hands of an angry God. You are a saint in the arms of a loving Father! Jesus bore all your sins so you would not have to bear them (1 Peter 2:24). You're saved from the wrath of God, and you now have peace with Him (Romans 5:9).

When tough circumstances come your way, you need to know they are never God's punishment. The world comes at you, but Christ is working in you. God is for you, never against you. God's discipline is training for your future, not punishment for your past.

PART 5

ARE YOU YOUR OWN WORST ENEMY?

CHAPTER 35

Kelly intercepted me as I was walking out of the room after a conference session I'd been giving. "You've ruined my prayer life!" she said.

Surprised, I stopped dead—but then I saw the twinkle in her eye. "What do you mean?" I asked, intrigued.

"Well, my prayer life used to be filled with asking God for things, even begging. I especially spent a lot of time asking God for forgiveness. That dominated my prayers for years. Now, I'm finding myself praying totally differently . . . and for other people! Can you believe that?" Kelly laughed.

Of course, I was relieved to understand what she meant. I replied sincerely, "That's great to hear. I wasn't sure what you were going to say at first when you said I ruined your prayer life."

We shared a laugh, and then she said, "There's more. I actually find myself sinning less now and without trying."

"Really?" I inquired—not surprised anymore, but still curious.

"Yes. The more I learn about God's grace, it just makes me realize He loves me," she said. "I no longer feel distant and unimportant to Him the way I once did. Plus, you talk about the new heart and the new desires we have. Once I started believing my newness in Christ, some of the old ways I used to think just sort of disappeared, without me even trying.

"It's hard to explain," she concluded, grasping for the words. "But let's just say . . . grace works!"

"That's awesome!" I exclaimed. "You're definitely the first person who has ever told me I ruined their prayer life. But this is not the first time I've heard somebody say learning about God's grace and new identity in Christ helped them get free from their past."

I had one last question for her. "What was it that helped you the most?" I asked.

"Realizing that I died with Jesus," Kelly replied. "You called it the neglected half of the Gospel. I see what you mean.

"Like you say, I signed my death certificate. I attended my own funeral!" she said with a radiant smile, "I realized I'm dead to those old thoughts. Now, I'm just relaxing and living under grace. I never knew it could be like this."

Why Not Just Sin?

In Romans, Paul asks a peculiar question: Should we go on sinning so grace may increase? A legalist would never ask this question. In their minds, grace does not increase! Should we go on sinning? "No," they would exclaim, "because you'll lose your salvation. No, because then you're out of fellowship. No, because you'll fall out of God's will."

On and on it goes with the scare tactics to keep people from sinning. But Paul's answer to this outrageous question is quite different. Should we go on sinning so grace may increase? He says "no," and here's why:

> *What shall we say, then? Shall we go on sinning so that grace may increase? By no means!* **We are those who have died to sin; how can we live in it any longer?** *Or don't you know . . . ?* (Romans 6:1–3a)

Paul's reason for you not continuing in sin relates to *your* death with Christ. That's interesting. As Kelly was pointing out, "Jesus died for your sins" is only half of the Gospel. "You died with Jesus" is the other half.

Here, Paul doesn't bring out any other reason to avoid sin. The fact that you were crucified, buried, and raised with Christ is the main reason not to go on sinning. He's telling you you're not made for sin. He literally asks: "How can we live in it any longer?" It's almost like it's impossible—given your new self, your new default setting, your new tendency. You want what God wants now.

A lot of people are scared of too much grace: "You're just saying I can go out and do whatever I want!" They're afraid of what they want. They're afraid that in an atmosphere of freedom, they will want to sin and then run wild.

But if they're in Christ, is that true? Romans 6 says we've become obedient from the heart, and we're now slaves of righteousness (verses 17–18). Apparently, God is not afraid of what we want. He's not afraid of what we'll end up doing under grace.

I'm not saying sin has died. Sin is very much alive, but we have died to sin's power. Big difference! So we still experience the presence of sin. We hear its voice, but it holds no real control over us. It's all bark and no bite. This is what it means to be dead to sin and alive to God.

God Is Not Naïve!

This radical exchange of personhood was essential for you. After all, God's grace won't work for just anybody. If you were still the old self and God put you under grace and forgave all your sins, it would be an absolute disaster. Without new desires, the whole thing makes no sense. Absolute freedom coupled with a sinful heart leads to a nightmare of a Christian life.

God was not naïve. He crucified you with Christ (Galatians 2:20). He caused you to die to the power of sin (Romans 6:2, 7, 12). God did this so you could be resurrected as a new creation with a new, obedient heart (2 Corinthians 5:17; Romans 6:17).

The Bottom Line

The grace message doesn't just mean you're totally forgiven, eternally secure, and unconditionally loved. There's more to it.

What happened to Jesus also happened to you—crucified, buried, and raised. By grace, you've been given a new heart, a new spirit, and God's Spirit. By grace, you've been equipped and empowered to live an upright life (Titus 2:11–12). Being afraid of too much grace is like being afraid of too much victory over sin.

Put another way: The grace message is not just freedom. It's freedom *and* a brand-new identity. James says if you're not acting like a doer of the Word, it's because you've forgotten what kind of person you are:

> *Anyone who listens to the word but **does not do what it** **says** is like someone who looks at his face in a mirror and, after looking at himself, goes away and **immediately forgets what he looks like***. (James 1:23–24)

Apparently, the answer to your struggle with sin is to take a long look in the mirror of God's Word. You need to remember who you are.

CHAPTER 36

"We're all made in the image of God." Maybe you've heard that. But here's the thing:

It's not *entirely* true.

The Bible tells us those first humans were created in God's image. However, something happened at the fall. Spiritual life was lost, and a line of humans born in the image of Adam followed:

> *This is the written account of Adam's family line.* **When God created mankind, he made them in the likeness of God.** *He created them male and female and blessed them. And he named them "Mankind" when they were created.* **When Adam had lived 130 years, he had a son in his own likeness, in his own image;** *and he named him Seth.* (Genesis 5:1–3)

While Adam and Eve were created perfect in the image of God, all of that changed. They ate of the fruit and went rogue, losing spiritual life. Satan seduced them and got away with "identity theft."

Then Adam and Eve had children, and their children were born *in the image of Adam*. They were fallen. Likewise, we too were born in the image of Adam. This is why we need to be reborn.

Romans 5 says sin entered the world, and humanity died. Condemnation was brought on everyone. We all became sinners by nature (Romans 5:12–19). Now, as born-again believers, we've been recreated in Christ, and we're experiencing a renewal in His image (Colossians 3:10). But originally, we were born in the image of Adam.

Identity always comes *by birth*.

In Adam. In Christ.

It's not about what you're doing; it's about who you're in.

First Corinthians 15:22 says that in Adam all die, and in Christ all are made alive. "Location, location, location," just like the realtors say. It's all about location. Everyone is somewhere spiritually, either dead in Adam or alive in Christ.

It's not just about our birth in Adam; it's about our resulting spiritual bloodline. Adam and Eve died spiritually and then had children: Cain, Abel, Seth, etc. Those children inherited a spiritual bloodline of death. We too were born in the spiritual bloodline of Adam.

We are who we are by *birth*, not by behavior. We could try to act differently—more like Jesus. But apart from a radical transfer into a new spiritual bloodline, we had no hope. We had to be moved out of Adam and into Christ. At salvation, that happened. We were transported from Adam's spiritual lineage, taken across a great chasm, and placed into Jesus forever.

As a result, we're no longer in the flesh (Romans 8:9). We're in the Spirit. This is what gives us a brand-new spiritual "bloodline" and nature. We don't get our identity from being in church on Sunday. We get our identity from being in Christ forever.

At salvation, God rips out our heart of stone and gives us a new heart. He gives us a new spirit, and He gives us His Spirit. This incredible transfer and heart surgery at the core of our being are what give us this new identity. And once we're aware of this transfer into Christ, we start seeing it all over the place in the New Testament:

> *For he has rescued us from the dominion of darkness and* **brought us into** *the kingdom of the Son he loves.* (Colossians 1:13)

> *It is because of him that you are* **in Christ Jesus**, *who has become for us wisdom from God—that is, our righteousness, holiness and redemption.* (1 Corinthians 1:30)

Your Journey into Death and Resurrection

There's more to it than being presently "in Christ." God shows us exactly how we became new in the first place. Understanding the journey involves attending our own spiritual funeral and signing our own death certificate.

*Or don't you know that all of us who were baptized into Christ Jesus were **baptized into his death**? We were therefore **buried with him** through baptism into death in order that, **just as Christ was raised** from the dead through the glory of the Father, **we too may live a new life**.* (Romans 6:3–4)

Spiritually, we were inserted into Christ and crucified with Him. Then we were buried with Him. But God didn't leave us in the tomb. He raised us up with Christ and seated us with Him in heavenly places (Ephesians 2:6). Now we've got the best seat in the house!

Christianity is like dying and waking up the next day a brand-new person. That's the true message of Christianity. It's not about behavior modification; it's about God's taking a spiritual syringe and extracting your old self and injecting you with a new one. This is what happened to you on the day you were born again. You couldn't be born again without dying first.

*For we know that **our old self was crucified with him** so that the body ruled by sin might be done away with, that we should no longer be slaves to sin—because **anyone who has died has been set free from sin**.* (Romans 6:6–7)

*Do not lie to each other, since **you have taken off your old self with its practices, and have put on the new self**, which is being renewed in knowledge in the image of its Creator.* (Colossians 3:9–10)

The Neglected Half

This is the neglected half of the Gospel. The first half is that Jesus died for you. The second half is that you died with Jesus. And God didn't leave you dead and buried. He raised you up and permanently bonded you together with Jesus:

> *Therefore, if **you have been raised with Christ**, keep seeking the things that are above, where Christ is, seated at the right hand of God. Set your minds on the things that are above, not on the things that are on earth. **For you have died, and your life is hidden with Christ in God**.* (Colossians 3:1–3)

Ephesians 2 says you're raised and seated in Heaven with Jesus. *Someday you're going where you're already seated.* You're new and heavenly on the inside, and someday you'll have the body to go with it.

Realizing you don't have to "die" every day is a big deal. Growing up, I heard it all: *You have to die to self. You have to sacrifice yourself every day. And you have to be careful not to crawl off that altar!*

First, there's no altar. The cross replaced all altars. Second, it's finished. Your old self died, and you're the new self. Don't expect the new self to die. It will never die. That's the whole point of having eternal life. So we can drop the morbid "martyr syndrome" and begin to enjoy life to the fullest with Jesus every day.

Maybe this is why God chose crucifixion among all forms of death. Crucifixion is unique in that you can't really do it to yourself. After you've nailed one hand up, where would you go from there? Crucifixion has to be done to you, and that's exactly what we find in Scripture:

> But **by His doing you are in Christ Jesus**, *who became to us wisdom from God, and righteousness and sancti-fication, and redemption.* (1 Corinthians 1:30)

God is the one who put you in Christ. He's the one who did the crucifying. Jesus's death was once for all. You died to sin in the same way: once for all (Romans 6:10–11). God doesn't want you to believe you need to kill yourself off every day or die to sin more. God already did it for you. It's finished, so you don't have to finish it.

Now, you can discover who you are in Christ and be yourself!

CHAPTER 37

I often catch up on my emails early in the morning, and sometimes I forget to have coffee first. One morning, I woke up to this zinger. The timestamp was from a few hours earlier, so it seemed someone had gotten themselves worked up late at night or very early in the morning:

> *You ignore the fact that the Christian life is one of daily crucifixion. Jesus Himself told us to take up our cross, and Paul said he died daily. We follow Jesus into death every single day as we lay down our lives on the altar. It is costly to deny ourselves on a daily basis and to live a life of sacrifice for God. You are encouraging people to be self-indulgent and lazy. The grace you teach will cause people to please themselves rather than Christ.*

Ouch. That's a great way to wake up, huh?

Take Up Your Cross?

Jesus did say if anyone wanted to follow Him, they had to deny themselves, take up their cross, and lose their life:

> *Then he called the crowd to him along with his disciples and said:* ***"Whoever wants to be my disciple must deny themselves and take up their cross and follow me.*** *For whoever wants to save their life will lose it, but whoever loses their life for me and for the gospel will save it. What good is it for someone to gain the whole world, yet forfeit their soul?"* (Mark 8:34–36)

So, should you get busy denying yourself? No. Jesus taught this to an unregenerate Jewish audience. This already happened to you at salvation. You admitted your old life wasn't worth living, and you wanted new life in Jesus. You denied your old self, took up your cross spiritually, and followed Jesus into death. You lost your former self. Now you have a new life and a new self.

There's no reason to deny the new self. Instead, recognize you are the new self.

Don't deny yourself. Be yourself!

Take Up Your Cross "Daily"?

Cynthia heard my teaching on Jesus's invitation to die, and she wrote in to ask: "Someone quoted the Scripture in

Luke 9 about taking up your cross *daily*. I thought I was already crucified. I'm not really trying to prove anyone wrong here, but I wonder what this Scripture in Luke means. Didn't Jesus's invitation to them to die mean salvation? Or is it about a daily choice to die to self?"

Luke presents us with an interesting phrase, "take up your cross *daily*" (Luke 9:23). In Matthew 16 and Mark 8, it merely says "take up your cross" without the word "daily." So what's going on in Luke? Do Christians need to die every day or not?

First, the word "daily" doesn't even appear in the earliest manuscripts of Luke 9. Some scholars propose the word "daily" was added to later manuscripts of Luke by a scribe who had in mind Paul's statement in 1 Corinthians 15 about dying daily (which we'll address next). In addition, the word "daily" doesn't appear in the manuscripts of Matthew and Mark which recount the same teaching of Jesus. This should tell you something!

Second, the new self doesn't need to be killed daily. God is *not* trying to slowly kill you off. He already did. At salvation, you were placed into Christ's death, burial, and resurrection.

Luke 9 is like the other accounts in Matthew and Mark. Jesus is saying you had to lose your old life to gain a new one. You followed Jesus. Where? To Calvary. Why? To die. Your old self was crucified with Christ (Galatians 2:20; Romans 6:6). Death and resurrection are what occurred in you the moment you were placed into Christ.

Now, you can wake up daily and count yourself dead to sin and alive to God. You don't need to kill you. You don't need to get rid of you. You're not the old self anymore. You're the new self. You can be yourself and express Jesus at the exact same time.

But Paul Died Daily!

If we don't have to die anymore, then why does Paul say, "I die daily"?

*And as for us, why do we **endanger** ourselves every hour? I face death every day—yes, just as surely as I boast about you in Christ Jesus our Lord. If I fought **wild beasts** in Ephesus with no more than human hopes, what have I gained?* (1 Corinthians 15:30–32a)

You may hear people quoting "I die daily" to justify a morbid get-rid-of-yourself theology. But did you notice that's not the meaning at all? Paul was talking about the physical danger he encountered every day as an apostle. He fought wild animals in Ephesus. He was out on the road traveling across the Gentile world to proclaim the Gospel. He faced all kinds of opposition. "I die daily" refers to the troubles he experienced. It's not about Paul's trying to kill himself spiritually because he's so sinful.

A Firm Put-Off

What about in Ephesians, where it says you were taught to put off your old self?

That, however, is not the way of life you learned when **you heard about Christ and were taught in him** *in accordance with the truth that is in Jesus.*

You were taught, with regard to your former way of life, to put off your old self, *which is being corrupted by its deceitful desires; to be made new in the attitude of your minds; and* **to put on the new self,** *created to be like God in true righteousness and holiness.* (Ephesians 4:20–24)

The verbs "to put off" and "to put on" here are infinitives. They have no time reference. They are not past, present, or future. Therefore, you have to look at the context (in the previous phrase) to determine what time they refer to. Paul is saying when they heard the Gospel, they were taught (past tense) to put off their old self and to put on their new self. That's what they were taught when they heard the Gospel for the first time—and they responded to it and were saved.

Still doubting? Paul expresses this same idea in Colossians using past tense, which makes it crystal clear:

Do not lie to each other, since **you have taken off your old self** *with its practices and* **have put on the new self,** *which is being renewed in knowledge in the image of its Creator.* (Colossians 3:9–10)

The taking off and the putting on of your new self is something that already happened at salvation. This means you don't have to get your old self to die off. It's already dead.

Don't try to "die." Count yourself alive to God!

The Bottom Line

When you were an unbeliever, your old self was alive and controlled by sin. But you died with Christ so that bond with sin would be broken. That way, you would no longer be controlled by sin's power. And you were then resurrected as a new self.

Now, even though the voice of sin is still present, it holds no real power over you. Sin is not dead, but you are dead to sin. The power of sin is all bark and no bite. The evil one cannot touch you, and you can rightfully count yourself dead to sin and alive to God.

> *For we know that our old self was crucified with him so that the body ruled by sin might be done away with, that **we should no longer be slaves to sin**—because **anyone who has died has been set free from sin**.* (Romans 6:6–7)

> *In the same way, **count yourselves dead to sin but alive to God in Christ Jesus**.* (Romans 6:11)

This isn't about you naming or claiming something to make it true. This is about you living in the reality that you don't want to sin. That's right: *You don't really want to sin.* You may feel you do, but you don't. You have a new default setting. You have a new normal. You're allergic to sin and addicted to righteousness!

CHAPTER 38

I love getting first-time callers on our weeknight radio program. They often have questions they've been wondering about for a long time, then happen upon our program and decide to call in. Philip from Manitoba was one of these callers. His question was about something he'd heard a lot, and maybe you've heard it too.

He began, "I'm often told that, as Christians, before we start our day, we should pray that we die to self that day. So, I just want to know if you could clarify that a little bit. I don't believe that means we're supposed to die, because we've already been crucified with Christ. So, what does that mean? And should we be praying this every day?"

"That's an important question," I said. "Do we need to wake up every day and start with a little prayer like, 'God, kill me'? Do we begin living each day by dying? Is that actually what the New Testament teaches?"

In short, I told him, the answer is *no*. The idea of dying to self every day sounds ominous and religious and sacrificial. It might even sound "Christian" to the masses. But how many times does the phrase "die to self" appear in the Bible? Zero. That's right. It never appears once. It may be in the Bible Belt, but it's not in the Bible!

Galatians 2:20 says you've been crucified with Christ. Romans 6 says your old self died. Colossians 2 says you died with Jesus. Ephesians 2 says you've already been raised from the dead with Christ. So how much more dying do you need to be doing? None.

We call ourselves new creations and say we have a new identity in Christ. Then, five minutes later, we say we need to die to ourselves. That's talking out of both sides of our mouths. The new self doesn't need to die to self.

We say we keep crawling off the altar and all of that. Well, there are no altars. There's only the cross, and we already died on it with Jesus. We need to stop trying to die and get busy living in union with Christ.

"That makes sense," Phillip said, relieved. "But now I have another question: If my old self is already dead, then why do I still sin?"

Why Do You Still Sin?

Here's the rub: Your old self is dead, buried, and gone. You're the new self, but obviously you still commit sins. So why do you still sin?

Over the years, I've heard it all. Some say you're "positionally" dead to sin but not experientially dead to it. Others say you're progressively dying to sin.

What's really going on? If your old self is dead, buried, and gone, then why do you still struggle?

I want to assure you there's a clear answer. But before we get there, think about this: If we can adequately explain why you still sin, are you willing to more fully believe you're new and righteous at the core?

Let's start by exposing some faulty explanations. Here's one: You still sin because you're a sinner by nature. If that were true, then you're set up for failure from the start. You're wicked, but you're supposed to live holy. You're sinful, but you're supposed to live righteously. Your heart agrees with Satan, but you're supposed to please God. Imagine it. Some of us don't have to imagine it, because this is exactly the apparent contradiction we've lived with far too long.

Here's another faulty explanation: You still sin because you're progressively dying to self. You haven't gotten rid of your self yet. This is even worse! You're not just being invited to believe you're evil yet supposed to live as though you're good. It goes further than that. You're invited to participate in *the destruction of your very self.*

You're supposed to kill yourself spiritually? How morbid is that! Yet so many have accepted the "die to self" theology, even though the expression is nowhere to be found in the Bible. Still, lots of Christian messaging has been built on this erroneous idea.

A Better Explanation

None of these are good explanations for why you still sin. You're not a dirty, rotten sinner anymore. You don't need to progressively tear down or kill your spiritual self. What Jesus already did for you is a lot better than any of that.

Here's the deal: We've almost got this thing completely backwards. Yes, backwards. We say the problem is S-E-L-F, when our real opponent is F-L-E-S-H.

The problem is not your actual self. Your old self died (Romans 6:6). You're the new self (Colossians 3:10). You're alive to God (Romans 6:11). However, you do struggle with something called "the flesh."

So what is the flesh?

The flesh, in Greek (*sarx*), is a way to think (Romans 8:5–6; Colossians 3:2), or a way to walk (Galatians 5:16). The flesh is that "stinking thinking" in your memory banks. You can still think in old ways or act in old ways, even though you're not the old self. So the flesh is a *way*, but the flesh is not you.

For several decades, the NIV Bible translated the Greek word *sarx* as "sinful nature." As a result, innumerable Christians presumed they had a new nature and a sinful nature at the same time. My first book, *The Naked Gospel*, was published by Zondervan, which also produced the NIV Bible. In my book, I discussed the problem with translating *sarx* as "sinful nature." During the editing process, my editor reached out to me to ask about the issue and understand it better. He communicated my concerns about *sarx* to Zondervan. I found out years later from the head of the NIV committee that I wasn't the only one to raise the issue. To their credit, Zondervan released the next edition of the NIV Bible with *sarx* translated as "flesh" instead of "sinful nature" in most instances.

Score another victory for the truth!

You might think this is just semantics. But if your spiritual nature is sinful, then God is essentially asking you to go against yourself for decades until you hit Heaven. You can't do it. It makes the Christian life impossible. But thank God for the truth: When you say *no* to the flesh, you're saying *yes* to your self. You're the new self! The flesh is your opponent— those old ways of thinking and acting that your new heart detests.

The flesh is not you. The flesh is not even part of who you really are.

You're not fighting a civil war against yourself. You're not a house divided. Yes, you have some "stinking thinking" to deal with every day, but it goes against your heart and your spiritual nature.

*Therefore, if anyone is in Christ, **the new creation** has come: **The old has gone, the new is here!*** (2 Corinthians 5:17)

CHAPTER 39

Sarita wanted to talk about something with me. "It might not seem like that big of a deal," she said shamefacedly, "but it's something I don't feel right about. And the problem is that I just can't seem to stop."

"What is it?" I asked.

"I find myself constantly talking badly about people at my work," Sarita said. "And it's not only that. If I've heard anything about someone, even if they told me themselves and asked me not to share it, I end up spilling the beans. I can't keep my mouth shut, even though I feel terrible every time I do. I'm just tired of it, because I know I've hurt people."

"What do you think causes you to make this choice each time?" I asked.

"I've thought about it a lot. Part of it is that I feel closer to someone if we share something, a secret. And if it's something bad about another person, then honestly maybe I do it to feel better about me. I think well, at least I'm not doing *that.*"

"That's pretty insightful. It sounds like you've already thought through your reasons quite a bit," I said. "So, what are you seeing as the solution?"

"Like I said, I've tried to stop, and I can't, so I don't know that I have an answer yet," she said, discouraged.

"Sarita, what you're describing is the flesh," I explained.

"The flesh is that pattern of thinking we developed before we met Jesus. And it's still available to us. When we fall into those patterns of behavior as believers, we're never satisfied or fulfilled. It just frustrates us.

"Part of the answer is to simply *recognize* those fleshly cravings for an unhealthy closeness to another person or the fleshly desire to look better in front of them. Those thoughts aren't really coming from you. In fact, they're designed to trap you in a cycle of behavior that you'll never be happy with— and that's exactly what has been happening."

"So then how do I keep from doing what the flesh wants?" she asked.

"Well, first, it's important to be aware of where this pull is coming from and what the agenda is," I said. "The goal is to make you frustrated, disappointed, and ultimately addicted to a cycle of unfulfilling behavior. But if you begin to believe your heart is not really in it and that you don't really want to do it, you can more easily reject those thoughts. Setting your mind on the truth of your true desires—to honor and respect people and to walk in dependence on God's Spirit and receive His counsel within you—that's how to avoid walking after the flesh."

"That makes sense," Sarita said as she thought about it more.

"Yes, it may make sense," I said, "but don't expect to walk out of here and never struggle just because you have a new perspective on fleshly thoughts coming at you. You still have to make those micro-choices in the moment. But knowing the source of the thoughts you receive and their agenda is a huge help. It gives you a leg up next time you confront the temptation. You'll realize you're not saying 'no' to yourself. You're saying 'no' to the flesh—a pattern of thinking that seeks to trap you in unhealthy behavior."

Digging Deeper

We've introduced the idea that you're actually on God's team all the time. Now, let's see if we can understand even better what the flesh really is and how it seeks to bring you down.

> *For consider your calling, brothers and sisters, that there were not many **wise** according to the flesh, not many **mighty**, not many **noble**.* (1 Corinthians 1:26 NASB)

Wisdom (smarts). Might (strength). Nobility (status). The flesh is the way we humans build these into our lives without looking to Christ. We fashion an identity around our intellectual attributes, physical attributes, or social status. Paul explained how he did this:

> *... although I myself could boast as having **confidence** even in the flesh. If anyone else thinks he is **confident** in the flesh, I have more reason: **circumcised** the eighth day,*

*of the **nation** of Israel, of the **tribe** of Benjamin, a Hebrew of Hebrews; as to the **Law**, a Pharisee; as to zeal, **a persecutor of the church**; as to the **righteousness which is in the Law**, found blameless.* (Philippians 3:4–6 NASB)

Paul built a flesh-based identity for himself around his birth, his nationality, his tribe, and his reputation. This helps us understand what the flesh really is. Obviously, it's not some sinister spiritual nature that a believer possesses. Rather, it's a way (a means, a strategy) to seek after worth and value from a worldly perspective.

Then Paul met Jesus. His identity changed. He then had infinite worth and value in Christ. But did his thoughts ever gravitate toward those old ways of gaining status? Sure! After he was saved, he could still walk *according to* the flesh at times, even though he was permanently located *in* the Spirit (Romans 8:9; Galatians 5:25).

Notice the type of flesh Paul describes in Philippians. It's positive and religious-looking, even impressive to his onlookers. In Galatians 5, we see the opposite: the dirty deeds of the flesh—sexual immorality, hatred, jealousy, and drunkenness (Galatians 5:19–21). So, we see two kinds of flesh—good-looking and bad-looking.

Here's another instance of good-looking flesh in Galatians:

*Are you so foolish? Having begun by the Spirit, are you now being **perfected by the flesh**?* (Galatians 3:3)

Again, the flesh doesn't always look bad. Here, the flesh is a way of seeking growth or self-improvement. It seeks to "perfect" you. Walking according to the flesh can be a good-looking substitute for trusting God's Spirit.

More on the Flesh

As we've seen, the flesh is a perspective, a mindset, a way to think or act. The flesh is in opposition to the work of God's Spirit in your life. The flesh is a means of building identity or status. You choose to put confidence in the flesh, or alternatively, in your union with Jesus. But the flesh is not you. The flesh is not your old self coming back to life. It's not your spiritual nature or self.

I'm a citizen of Texas. It's where I live. But I've been known to put on a New York accent or a Boston accent at times. Even though I might talk that way, I'm acting like someone I'm not. My talk doesn't define me.

In the same way, we're citizens of Heaven, and we live in God's Spirit. Even though we sometimes walk (or talk) after the flesh, it doesn't define us. In those moments, we're acting like someone we're not.

You have a new default setting—dependence on Christ. It's who you are. Being yourself and expressing Jesus at the exact same time—that's what you're designed for. God has the market cornered on true fulfillment, and nothing else will satisfy you.

Two Analogies

Here are two ways to better understand the flesh.

Every four or eight years, a new president moves into the White House. Often what you see next is a replacement of the policies of the former administration. This is a bit like what happens spiritually—our old self dies, and our new self moves in. *The flesh is the policies of the former administration.* The flesh is the ways we used to operate when we didn't know Jesus. We can still fall back on those strategies, but slowly they're being replaced with new and better "policies" as we grow in God's grace and get our minds renewed.

Another way to understand the flesh is to think about a computer. You buy a brand-new laptop, and you take it home. You open the box and within five minutes, it says you need a software update. But you just bought it! Why in the world does it need a software update?

The hardware is brand-new, but the software is out of date. Likewise, when you're born again, you get shiny, new "heartware." But you still need software updates—the renewing of the mind. *The flesh is like out-of-date software trying to run alongside your new spiritual heartware.*

How Do You Fight the Flesh?

How do you fight the flesh? The answer may surprise you! It doesn't involve examining the flesh or focusing on the flesh at all. No, Paul teaches the opposite:

> *So, I say, **walk by the Spirit**, and you will **not** gratify the desires of the flesh.* (Galatians 5:16)

Your role in the fight is to walk by the Spirit. Simply keep your focus on Jesus. You don't have to examine and fight the flesh. You set your mind on things above (Colossians 3:2). As you do, you won't carry out the desires of the flesh.

> *If we **live** by the Spirit, let us also **walk** by the Spirit.* (Galatians 5:25 NASB)

This is godly common sense. Because Christ is your life, you're called to act that way. Because you're in a vine-and-branches relationship with Jesus, you're invited to think and act that way. If you live by the Spirit, why not walk by the Spirit? It's the most natural choice you could make given who you are and Who you're connected to.

CHAPTER 40

Charise messaged me after watching our radio program to ask an uncomfortable question. For years, she'd been reading all kinds of historical dramas with lots of sex in them. In many ways, she found the characters in the books to be more attractive and more interesting than her husband. This led her into a world of fantasy that she felt significant shame about.

"I'm pretty sure it's not okay," she said, "I just don't know what to do. I can't seem to stop. I feel tremendous guilt about it, and it's hurting my marriage for sure. I can't even enjoy being with my husband anymore. I feel like he just doesn't measure up."

"What if I told you those thoughts and desires don't even come from you?" I asked.

"I'd say they certainly feel like me," Charise fired back, almost immediately.

"Yes, I know what you mean, but in this case there's something you don't know, and you're being tricked," I wrote. "You're believing the lie that you want to fantasize and build a pretend world of romance to live in. This is how the enemy gets you distracted and erodes the joy in your marriage."

"I hear you, but I don't think we can blame the whole thing on demons or something like that. I'm the one who made bad choices along the way," she replied, concerned that I was taking away her personal responsibility.

"That's right, you made choices, for sure," I said. "But where did those thoughts and desires originate from? That's the question. What I'm saying is a power called 'sin' offered you those thoughts, and you chose to accept them as your own. But the thoughts didn't originate with you, and they're not what you really want."

"I just want to make sure I'm taking credit for what I've done," she responded.

"Credit?" I pondered. "Well, you can take responsibility for your choices and the consequences. But please don't take credit for generating those sinful thoughts. The whole point of understanding your new identity in Christ is to realize you have a new heart, an obedient heart. You have a new spiritual nature, and sin doesn't originate with you. Yes, the power called 'sin' is at work in you to deceive you, but sin is not you. This makes you more responsible for your choices, not less."

"How so?" she asked next.

"Well, if you're a lustful person by nature who wants to fantasize, then good luck saying 'no' to yourself for the next several decades until you hit Heaven," I explained. "But if you're new-hearted and godly at the core, then those fantasizing thoughts don't fit with you. You can reject them as not being your own. You can count yourself dead to sin and alive to God."

"I get it," she finally replied. "I guess I assumed any thought in my head is my own and that's where my heart is."

"No, not the case at all!" I exclaimed, "When it comes to sin, your heart is not in it. You've got a new heart. You're allergic to fantasy and addicted to truth. That's your nature now, and nothing else will satisfy."

That night, the light bulb went on for Charise. For the first time, she could see a new way to respond to a very old struggle.

The Power of Sin

It's not just the old patterns of thinking known as the flesh. A power called *sin* is feeding us thoughts every day. I'm not talking about "sins," plural. I'm talking about a parasite called "sin."

We see this parasitic force first mentioned in Genesis:

> *If you do what is right, will you not be accepted? But if you do not do what is right, **sin is crouching at your door; it desires to have you, but you must rule over it**.* (Genesis 4:7)

God is signaling to Cain that a power called "sin" has entered the fallen world. It seeks to take him by surprise and devour him. Again, this is not the verb "to sin." This is a noun, an entity, known as "sin." This same force shows up in Romans 7 when Paul is announcing his discovery of this force at work within him.

Definition of "Sin"

Vine's Complete Expository Dictionary of Old and New Testament Words says "sin" (Greek: *hamartia*) is a governing power with *person-like characteristics*. Person-like characteristics? Yes, this parasitic force called "sin" is intelligent and offers thoughts and ideas just like a person might. *Vine's* also notes that sin acts through the members of our body.

Romans 6:12 says, "[D]o not let *sin* reign in your mortal body so that you obey *its* evil desires." Where do the evil desires really come from? From sin.

The evil desires originate with the power of sin, not you. *However, we can easily mistake the thoughts offered by this parasite as being our own.* (Then, next thing you know, we're building a theology of needing to kill ourselves spiritually!)

God wants us to know the truth. He's calling us to rethink everything in terms of temptation. He has given us the mind of Christ (the Holy Spirit's counsel) to help us sort it out (1 Corinthians 2:16). He wants us to know: Like a parasite, sin operates in you, but it's not you.

A Deeper Look at Sin

Paul, formerly Saul of Tarsus, was living under the Law and trying his best not to covet other people's belongings. In the midst of this effort, he discovered a parasite (sin) working to enslave him. The result was coveting of every kind.

Two times, he makes it clear this entity (sin) had the power to override his efforts and put him in bondage. The power of sin was at work in him, but it was not him:

> *As it is, it is **no longer I** myself who do it, but it is **sin** living in me.* (Romans 7:17)

> *Now if I do what I do not want to do, it is **no longer I** who do it, but it is **sin** living in me that does it.* (Romans 7:20)

As an unregenerate Jewish man living under the Law, Saul discovered he was being controlled by this parasitic force. He says he was "unspiritual, sold as a slave to sin" (Romans 7:14).

Where exactly did this power gain access to him? Through his physical body. You see, because our bodies are part of a fallen world—and the power of sin has entered this world—then sin accesses our thought life through the body (specifically, the brain).

> *... but I see a different law **in the parts of my body** waging war against the law of my mind, and making me a prisoner of the law [principle, power] of sin, the law **which is in my body's parts**.* (Romans 7:23)

When you received Jesus, you didn't get a new body. So, sin still has access to offer messages to your brain. It's like sin is tapping your phone line and placing calls, and you've been paying the bill!

Can you see how the voice of this parasitic force could be mistaken for your old self?

The Bottom Line

If you haven't caught it yet, here's the great news: You're not fighting with yourself. It's not "the good you" versus "the bad you." Jesus said, "If a house is divided against itself, that house cannot stand" (Mark 3:25).

Thank God you're not a house divided. Yes, you still sin because of the flesh and the parasitic power called sin. These are your opponents, but they're not you. The war is not with yourself. The war is with sin, and you're *not* sin.

You're a child of God!

CHAPTER 41

One Sunday afternoon, Kayden from New York called our radio studio.

"You teach about sin, saying it is not us," Kayden said. "But isn't that just 'the devil made me do it'? Where does personal responsibility come in?"

You can see where Kayden's question is coming from. Twice in Romans 7, Paul says it's not him, but a parasite called sin.

Knowing about the power of sin makes you more responsible, not less. Here's the logic: "Hey, this is not even me. Why would I want a parasite to take over? Why would I want the power of sin to dominate if I can say 'no' to it? I'm dead to sin and alive to God. I don't have to let sin have its way!"

So it's the opposite of the "the devil made me do it." Instead, it's "I don't have to do it, and I don't want to do it. And the devil can't make me do it, because it didn't come from me in the first place!"

Factoring in the power of sin is not some sort of cop-out. When you understand your identity in Christ, it makes you more responsible for your choices, not less. Imagine if you were still a sinner by nature, a slave to sin. You'd have the greatest excuse in the world to sin: "I can't help it. It's my nature. I'm a sinner, so the most natural thing for me to do is sin. I can't escape my own desires!"

But now you know the truth. You're a slave of righteousness (Romans 6:18). You're allergic to sin. You're addicted to Jesus. You're going to prove this truth one way or another: by sinning and being miserable or by trusting Jesus and being fulfilled. Either way, you prove sin won't work for you. God has empowered you to live in a new and better way.

If You Don't Know . . .

If you don't realize this parasite is at work, you could start building an identity around the sinful thoughts you're getting: "I'm a gossip. I'm a critical person. I'm a pervert. I'm an alcoholic." Now, you may drink too much to drown your sorrows, to deal with your problems, to go into escapism, but *you are a child of God*. That's your identity, no matter how much you drink.

However, the enemy will heap on the accusations and condemnation: "You call yourself a Christian yet look at your thoughts! How could you be thinking this stuff? You must be backslidden! You're far away from God! You're out of fellowship! There's no way a real Christian would think these thoughts!"

That's the one-two punch of the enemy: Sin offers you the thought and then accuses you of having it. You end up wondering, "How can I be such a sincere, eager child of God but struggle so much with sin? How can I have true desires to please God, but get these thoughts flooding my head?" To make things worse, maybe in the back of your mind, there's this ten-out-of-ten perfect specimen of a Christian that never struggles. He's never tempted like you are and never has those thoughts. Then you feel even worse for the sinful ideas spinning through your mind.

What if you realized that not a single sinful thought originates with you? What if you recognized that every temptation comes from a force that opposes you? Wouldn't knowing the source of those thoughts help in the battle?

Even many theologians start with their experience of being tempted and then conclude their old self still must be active. What they're really experiencing are thoughts from the power of sin masquerading as their old self.

What if we knew the difference?

Seeing Others Differently

Ultimately, this message of new identity is not just about you. You can see your spouse, your friends, and your children the way God sees them as well. I've seen broken marriages and frayed relationships put back together when couples realized they were on the same page and shared the same heart. They also realized they shared a common enemy: sin.

Perhaps the husband had a struggle with pornography and grew to hate himself. The wife resented him for his problem and began to believe lies about herself—namely, that she didn't measure up.

When they both began to see their own righteousness and each other's, it made a difference. They realized where the lustful thoughts were coming from: a common enemy called sin. They also realized where the resentful and self-deprecating thoughts stemmed from. Together, they enjoyed the revelation that their common struggle was not against flesh and blood (Ephesians 6:12), but against an outside influence, a parasitic force—sin.

The Bottom Line

Your death to sin was not progressive. You've already died to sin. You can't be any more dead to sin.

*The death he died, **he died to sin once for all**; but the life he lives, he lives to God. In the **same way, count yourselves** dead to sin but alive to God in Christ Jesus.* (Romans 6:10–11)

Jesus died to sin once for all. You were in Him, and you died to sin once for all. Count yourself dead to sin "in the same way"—just like Jesus. You don't die to sin a little bit on Monday and a little bit more on Tuesday. Dying to sin doesn't happen with more time, prayer, Bible study, or church attendance. Dying to sin happens through crucifixion—once. You'll never be crucified with Christ again. So, you can drop the theology of trying to die to sin more over time. You're as dead to sin as you'll ever be. And because of the power of the indwelling Christ, you can say "no" to sin right here and now.

CHAPTER 42

One morning, I opened my mail to find a lengthy letter from Lara. It began this way:

I heard the Gospel and opened my heart to the Lord when I was young. Early on, I was on fire for God. I shared my faith. I brought people to church. I felt passionate about my relationship with Jesus.

But then something happened. It wasn't overnight. It was more like a slow decay. All the great feelings I once had about my relationship with God slowly dwindled. Now, I hardly feel much of anything, and to be honest, I wonder if I'm even saved anymore—or if I ever was.

The letter went on to describe how Lara had lost assurance of salvation. She had begun comparing her Christian "experience" with that of other believers. She had measured herself and determined she was not feeling enough. And the enemy was piling on with accusations: "If you were truly saved, you'd feel more. If you were truly saved, you'd experience more."

"You opened the door of your heart, and God promised to come in," I wrote back, "and you called upon the name of the Lord, and He promised to save you. He said that He would never leave you, and never forsake you, and nobody could snatch you out of His hand. Even when you're faithless (or feel nothing!), He remains faithful. Nothing separates you from His love."

I went on to emphasize that salvation isn't a feeling; it's a fact. Salvation isn't an "experience"; it's a promise for all who put their trust in Jesus Christ.

"I don't always feel forgiven either, but I am forgiven," I wrote, "and I don't always feel clean and close to God, but I am clean and close to Him. I feel all kinds of things as I ride the roller coaster of the soul up and down and all around. But my assurance is about the truthfulness of God. He's not a liar. He's a truth teller. So, when He promised to come in and save me forever, I need to believe Him, no matter what my emotions may be. That's what faith is. We walk by faith, not by feeling."

Lara's thought processes are not uncommon. You might think, "I feel nothing. I feel numb. I feel dirty and distant, therefore I must not be saved." We're all tempted to believe those lies, but it doesn't make them true. You can know you're saved because of the trustworthiness of God's promises, not because of what you feel or don't feel.

Theology of the Soul

Why do so many believers fail to understand their new identity in Christ?

I think it comes down to a "theology of the soul." What do I mean by that? Your soul is what houses your emotions. The soul is like an experience tank. It can go through anything: doubt, fear, and other emotional experiences. We ride the rollercoaster of the soul every day. But God calls us to worship Him in spirit and in truth (John 4:24).

So it's dangerous for us to develop a belief system based on what we might feel. Sure, it's tempting to believe what you feel is always reality. Remember, that's why some theologians start with the idea that they commit sins (and feel sinful) and therefore conclude their old self must still be around.

But once we realize there are influencers (the flesh and sin) causing our soul to experience thoughts and feelings that go against who we are, everything makes more sense. We can begin to walk by faith in the truth of who we really are in Christ, not by feeling.

The Truth about You!

You were recreated in Christ Jesus *for good works* (Ephesians 2:10). If that's what you were refashioned by God for, what does that say about your design? Romans 6:21 implies that sin is unnatural and unfruitful for you in every way. One great way for you to be miserable is to go out and sin. You'll discover you hate it every time!

Why? *Because you don't really want to sin.* That's right: God has rigged it so that you don't want to sin anymore.

> *No one who is born of God will continue to sin, because God's seed remains in them; they cannot go on sinning, because they have been born of God.* (1 John 3:9)

Apparently, you're going to have real trouble practicing sin. All kinds of alarms will go off inside you. It goes against your new default setting. It goes against the very fiber of your being. You have a new pattern and a new practice—a new tendency and a new trend. You can't just sin and love it anymore.

> *For the flesh sets its desire against the Spirit, and the Spirit against the flesh;* **for these are in opposition to one another, so that you may not do the things that you please.** (Galatians 5:17, NASB 1995)

Check out the two sides of this battle very carefully: the flesh and the Spirit. They oppose each other, but whose side are you on? You're on God's side. It's the flesh that's trying to drag you down. It wants to keep you from doing the things that truly please you.

I used to read this the wrong way, assuming the Spirit of God was keeping me from doing what I wanted (to sin). Some Bible translations even skew the meaning of this passage in that direction, claiming the Spirit keeps "you from doing whatever you want." But I don't read it with legalistic glasses on anymore. I see that I'm on God's team, and it's the flesh that is trying to keep me from doing the *beautiful* things I want to do.

I want what God wants.

This is even backed up by the Greek word *thélō* in Galatians 5:17. It doesn't merely mean "to want whatever." No, it means to want *what is best or optimal*. In fact, the same root is used to describe what *God* wants in extending His "best offer" to humanity. Galatians 5:17 is conveying that the flesh is warring against you to keep you from doing the optimal, godly things you truly desire. How amazing is that insight!

> *Dear friends, I urge you, as foreigners and exiles, to abstain from **sinful desires**, which wage war **against** your soul.* (1 Peter 2:11)

Growing up, I heard sin was what the world did, and they were living it up. They were having a great time. But I shouldn't sin like them, because I'm a Christian.

Now, I see things very differently. Sin is poisonous and damaging, and my Father isn't holding out on me. He's protecting me from experiencing constant disaster. He wants me to be fulfilled in every way.

Freedom from sin is freedom from misery.

CHAPTER 43

I was meeting with Rachel and Craig. She wanted to talk about problems they were having with their marriage.

"Craig has cheated on me three different times since we've been married!" Rachel said as tears ran down her cheeks, "and even when we were engaged, I'm pretty sure he was with other women. I've tried to move beyond this, but I just can't."

At this point, Craig intervened. "I know this was wrong," he said, "and I'm very ashamed of it. I didn't have a relationship with God back then, and that was just the world I'd grown up in, so I didn't understand why it was a big deal. Now I do, though, and I've apologized and promised Rachel I'll never do it again. But we can't seem to move forward. We're stuck."

"How do you feel about Craig now, Rachel?" I asked.

"I still feel betrayed. I feel stupid for trusting him, again and again," Rachel said. "And I feel like garbage, as if I have no value. He has never made me feel like I mattered. He doesn't even know how."

"So, these episodes of Craig's unfaithfulness have made you feel betrayed, stupid, and unvalued," I said. "That is very understandable.

"I think most people would agree, and even Craig would now, too: He should've been loyal to you. He should've been trustworthy. He should've valued you."

They both nodded, and I continued, "But Craig didn't do any of these, so in a sense he owes you a debt. And forgiveness is when you assess the damage and cancel the debt, releasing him from what he owes you," I explained.

"Forgiveness is a loaded word for me. I feel like I've forgiven him over and over. I've prayed for him. I have tried not to think badly about him. But I just can't stop," Rachel said.

"You don't understand, Rachel. This is for you," I explained. "This is for your benefit mainly, not his. This is about you going free. Praying for him is not forgiving him. Trying not to think badly about him is not forgiving him either.

"Forgiveness is when you cancel his debt so that you're no longer bound and controlled by things like bitterness and resentment," I concluded. "Again, this is for you mainly, not him."

"What if I can't find it in my heart to forgive?" she asked.

"God has already found it in your heart," I said. "He has told you through His Word that He gave you a new heart, an obedient heart, a righteous heart, a forgiving heart. Forgiveness is what you really want to do in this case, whether you feel it or not. If you will trust God in this, you'll find the freedom you're designed for."

Rachel thought about my words for a few seconds and then said, "Okay, I will choose to forgive him here and now, no matter what I'm feeling."

I walked Rachel through the process of forgiving her husband for his unfaithfulness. I took note of all the damage done, all the feelings felt, and all the debt owed. Then, together, we reviewed everything. Rachel chose to cancel Craig's debt. That day, she went free from all the scorekeeping that had kept her in bondage inside.

Forgiveness doesn't mean we sign up for more pain. Forgiveness doesn't mean we throw wisdom or common sense out the window. But it does mean we no longer allow thoughts of scorekeeping, bitterness, and resentment to control us. That's how we find health and move forward through the hurt in the way God designed.

It starts with recognizing what kind of heart you really have. You have a heart that will only be satisfied when you release others from their "debt" against you.

Your New (Forgiving!) Heart

When you're young, you're told you need to ask Jesus to live in your heart. Then within a decade or two, maybe you hear your heart is "deceitful above all things" and "desperately wicked" (Jeremiah 17:9 NKJV). Maybe you don't even think about the contradiction there.

Does Jesus live in dirty, sinful hearts?

Quoting the Old Testament out of context, some religious messaging convinces you that your heart is not right before God. Your heart must be tested and never trusted, they claim. You heart is hard, they say. You need to "get your heart right with the Lord."

But God had always planned for you to receive a new heart at salvation (Ezekiel 36:26), and it is a loving, obedient heart (Romans 6:17). The heart that was deceitful, wicked, and bitter was removed and replaced. God crossed your heart: He took your heart to the cross! You now have a new, obedient, and forgiving heart.

When it comes to bitterness and resentment, your heart's not in it. Forgiving others is your destiny, and nothing else will satisfy you.

Even when resentful thoughts hit you, you have a go-to place at the center of your being. You can take that "one-foot journey" from head to heart and make decisions from your new spiritual core. You can trust your heart. Your heart is always right with God, because He gave you a right heart.

> Each of you should give **what you have decided in your heart** to give, not reluctantly or under compulsion, for God loves a cheerful giver. (2 Corinthians 9:7)

You can give and live (and forgive!) from your heart. It's not only safe to do so, it's the way you're supposed to function. You experienced a circumcision of the heart for this very reason.

> No, a person is a Jew who is one inwardly; and circum- cision is **circumcision of the heart, by the Spirit**, not

by the written code. Such a person's praise is not from other people, but from God. (Romans 2:29)

Your new, loving heart also means *you don't need more love for God.* You have all the love for Him you'll ever need. Ephesians 6:24 says your love for Christ is "undying." You're a lover of God, whether you feel that love or not.

You may have heard countless sermons about how you need to love God more and prove your love for Him. But the truth is you love Him to the maximum possible degree. You can't love God any more than you already do. You'll never stop loving Him!

*Grace to all who love our Lord Jesus Christ **with an undying love**.* (Ephesians 6:24)

The Bottom Line

The bottom line is we don't have to do anything to become more forgiving or more loving. We simply need to recognize who God has made us in Jesus Christ. We are dead to hate and alive to the love of God. We are His workmanship. He did a perfect job handcrafting us just as He wants us to be!

*For we are **God's handiwork**, created in Christ Jesus to do good works, which God prepared in advance for us to do.* (Ephesians 2:10)

*But you are a chosen people, a royal priesthood, a holy nation, **God's special possession**, that you may declare* *the praises of him who called you out of darkness into his wonderful light.* (1 Peter 2:9)

CHAPTER 44

"I've been to several of your events over the last few years. I've been soaking the grace message in, but I still find some of it hard to believe," Esther admitted after one of our Saturday conferences.

"What part is the most difficult for you, Esther?" I asked.

"I get the forgiveness part and the idea of living under grace," she said. "All of that makes sense to me. But it's the 'being new' part that trips me up. I inevitably mess up every day and get things wrong, so it's tempting to believe I'm not any different than I was before."

"I know what you mean," I agreed, "and I don't think what you're describing is unusual. Often the hardest part of the grace message to believe is the part that pertains to you—your heart, your self, your nature. It's hard to buy into your newness when you're still getting sinful thoughts and your performance doesn't line up."

As Christians, though, I explained, we believe a lot of crazy things. We believe God said, "Let there be light" and spoke the world into being. We believe a flood engulfed the whole earth and one family was saved in an ark. We believe a man was swallowed by a whale and lived inside it for three days until he was spit up on the beach. We believe Jesus rose from the dead and then floated into the clouds to be reunited with His Father in Heaven. We believe a lot of crazy things!

"Why not believe one more crazy thing?" I asked her. "The same Bible that taught you all these crazy things also says you spiritually died with Jesus and were resurrected as a brand-new person at the core. The same Bible says just beneath your flesh and bones and everything you have called 'you', there's an invisible part of you that has been raised and seated with Christ. The old you was ripped out and replaced with someone spiritually compatible with Jesus. Now, you're a perfect fit with Him."

I asked Esther this, and I ask you too: Are you willing to reinterpret your entire thought life in light of this truth? Will you agree with God that every single sinful thought you receive is not from you? Will you agree to believe this even when sinful thoughts feel familiar and seem so much like you? This is what it means to walk by faith and to count yourself dead to sin and alive to God.

This Was Always the Plan!

All of this was prophesied in the Old Testament:

*I will give you **a new heart** and put **a new spirit** in you; I will remove from you your heart of stone and give you a heart of flesh. And I will put **my Spirit** in you and move you to follow my decrees and be careful to keep my laws.* (Ezekiel 36:26–27)

Notice the three things you received at salvation.

- **First, you got a new heart.** This means you received new spiritual passions and desires from God.
- **You also received a new spirit.** Remember, this happened as you were taken out of Adam and placed into Christ: crucified, buried, and raised to new life.
- **You also received God's Spirit.**

A lot of believers don't realize the difference between God's "Spirit" and your "spirit." Not only did you receive the Holy Spirit to dwell within you forever; you also received a new human spirit. This was important in making you compatible with Jesus. Jesus is not the new creation; you are!

You were recreated in Christ Jesus as holy and righteous and blameless at the core. You'll always be dependent on Christ within you, but it certainly helps that God gave you a heart and a spirit that are in perfect alignment with Him. He's your source and your strength, and you want what He wants.

*Therefore, if anyone is in Christ, **this person is a new creation**; the old things passed away; behold, new things have come.* (2 Corinthians 5:17)

You're a Christlike Saint!

This is why we are rightly called "saints," not sinners. We commit sins, but they don't define us. We're defined by our new spiritual birth. The word "sinner" appears all over the New Testament, but it never refers to a child of God.

We are saints who sometimes sin.

Maybe you've heard you're supposed to try to be "Christlike." And yes, I get it. Your attitudes and actions are lagging. You're still experiencing the renewing of the mind. We all are.

But what do you look like on the inside? If we were to cut you open on a spiritual operating table to examine your new heart and your new spirit, what would we see?

The truth is that you *are* Christlike.

> *This is how love is made complete among us so that we will have confidence on the day of judgment:* ***In this world we are like Jesus****. (1 John 4:17)

When God says you're "born of Him," what does that mean? When the Holy Spirit gives birth to you, making you "born of the Spirit," what does He give birth to if not someone who is Christlike? Yes, Spirit gives birth to spirit (John 3:6). So, because of your new birth, you are Christlike at the heart level. That's some serious inspiration for Christlike attitudes and actions!

Chief of Sinners?

DeAndre reached out to me on social media to ask this question: "Paul called himself the 'chief of sinners,' but you say we are saints who sometimes sin. Is 'sinner' not a good label for Christians? I do call my family and myself 'saints,' but the 'chief of sinners' passage is unclear to me. What did Paul mean when he called himself that?"

"Yes, Paul did call himself 'chief of sinners,'" I agreed. "But he was referring to his past, before salvation, as an assassin of the church. He was 'a blasphemer and a persecutor and a violent man,' according to 1 Timothy 1:13."

I went on to explain that Paul was highlighting his track record of killing Christians before he met Jesus on that Damascus Road. Paul was showcasing how much mercy God had lavished on him, even though he was an opponent of the Gospel.

"Remember," I told DeAndre, "this is the same Paul who stood by and gave hearty approval at the stoning of Stephen. He watched the torture of many other believers too, I'm sure. But at salvation, Paul was crucified and buried and raised with Christ. He went on to write more New Testament letters than anyone else. That tells you something. God was willing to forgive and transform a person who stood in direct opposition to His grace."

The Bottom Line

Paul called himself the "chief of sinners," but he was referring to his track record in killing Christians before his salvation. In his mind, he had hit a world record in terms of sinning. So the last thing we should be doing is pulling this verse out of context and calling ourselves "chiefs of sinners" instead of saints.

If Jack Nicklaus were to claim he is the greatest golfer of all time, it doesn't mean he currently plays on tour. He doesn't. But he set so many records that he could rightly call himself the chief of golfers.

Paul felt the same way. Even though he was no longer a sinner by nature, he formerly engaged in so much evil against the Church that he set records in his own mind. To him, it was shocking that God would show him so much grace and transform him into a saint.

Just like Paul, you too have been crucified and raised with Christ. You've had a DNA swap, a heart transplant, a surgery at the core of your being that has fundamentally changed who you are.

You're not a sinner by nature anymore. You're a saint who sometimes sins.

CHAPTER 45

"I eat too much," Dan said, "I can't put it any other way. I eat too much, and then I repent, but then I just do it again. The more I put a ban on certain foods, the more I end up bingeing on them later."

"What do you think are the reasons for your overeating?" I asked.

"Sometimes, I'm just bored, so it's mindless eating even when I'm not hungry. Sometimes, I do eat to cope with stress, I think. I've analyzed it a thousand times, and no matter what I come up with, it just doesn't change."

"What do you feel about it?" I asked.

"Oh, I'm constantly overloaded with guilt and shame about it. I'm embarrassed to go outside, to be with people, because of my weight. I'm afraid of what they might label me, so it makes me want to completely avoid contact."

"And you've tried limiting certain foods from your diet?" I asked.

"Yes, but like I said, it really only makes things worse. It seems like the more I ban, the more I'm triggered to eat even more."

"Dan, I'm certainly not a diet specialist, and I could stand to exercise more and lose a few pounds myself," I said. "There are lots of reasons people end up overweight, and some of those reasons are unavoidable. But I'll share with you what I've learned about temptation in general if you'd like."

"Yes, I know I have to be the one to make the tough choices, but I just feel like there's something missing in the equation—maybe it's spiritual, maybe it's not," he replied.

"Well, here's what I do know," I said. "Many believers are unaware of sin as a power at work within them seeking to deceive them. Most believers think all their thoughts come from them. They don't realize how sin can sound and feel like them even when it's not them. As a result, they end up doing what they don't want to do.

"Now, there may be more to your situation—physical issues, health concerns—I don't know," I continued. "But I do want you to be aware that the power of sin is happy to feed you thoughts of guilt and shame about yourself and then have you look to overeating as a band-aid for that. Then, when you try to ban certain foods from your diet, you're putting yourself under law and that only excites sin. It never achieves the effect you're looking for."

"So, then what am I supposed to do? Just have no boundaries and eat whatever I want?" Dan asked.

"Well, how much do you want to eat? And when do you want to stop?" I asked.

"I want to eat only when I'm hungry, and then I want to stop when I'm full," he answered.

"There you go," I replied. "That's your true desire. Everything else that hits your head is questionable. So, it's wise of you to ask, 'Where is this thought coming from and what is it seeking to do to me?' In asking this question, you're simply being aware of your true desires and remembering that not all the thoughts you get are in line with what you really want."

"It's like you've said before: the power of sin is in me, but it's not me," he said thoughtfully.

"Exactly," I agreed. I then elaborated on this:

"The guilty and condemning thoughts are not of you and not of God. God doesn't want you thinking that way about yourself. The shameful thoughts are not of Him. Likewise, the thoughts of eating to feel better about yourself are not from you either. They don't make any sense, since you can already feel great about yourself. You're holy and righteous and blameless and off-the-charts awesome. That's God's truth about you. That's what you need to come back to in every moment, no matter how much you're eating or not eating. And I would encourage you to rethink the restrictions or bans you're putting on certain foods. You may continue to find they have the opposite effect from what you desire. Put your attention on your righteousness and God's delight in you. You may find this is the healing balm you've been looking for."

Righteousness

Righteousness. It's a topic you may not often connect to your life struggles. But righteousness is incredibly relevant and speaks to what you believe about yourself, your importance, your value. Your understanding of your righteousness also impacts the degree to which you're deceived by the power of sin into entertaining alternative ways of finding fulfillment for yourself.

Are you as righteous as me? Are you as righteous as Mother Teresa or Billy Graham? Are you as righteous as the Apostle Paul? Are you as righteous as Jesus?

I'll sometimes ask a conference audience to raise their hands in response to these questions. They quickly assert they're as righteous as me. That's a no-brainer! But as we progress through Mother Teresa, Billy Graham, the Apostle Paul, and Jesus, something happens. Fewer hands are raised with each turn, and hardly any remain raised when it comes to being as righteous as Jesus.

What's going on there? We are hesitant even though we believe we were made righteous by grace through faith? Yes, we still get confused about how righteous we are and how we got this way.

To understand this better, let's think about how we became sinners. How many sins did you commit to become a sinner? Some people respond, "It only took one sin!" But the truth is it took zero sins. You were *born* a sinner.

Remember: We are who we are by birth, not by what we do. This is precisely what makes us righteous. We're righteous by new birth, not by behavior. Thinking through this helps us understand God's perspective better. We're as righteous as

Jesus (1 John 3:7; 2 Corinthians 5:21). In fact, there are no partially righteous people on the planet. Anyone who is righteous at all is as righteous as Jesus.

This is why we shouldn't be barking orders about behavior improvement to an unbelieving world. They need righteousness by new birth, not behavior reform. Likewise, we need to be highlighting our new birth to the Christian world today, not merely trying to get them to act better. Once we realize we're righteous by new birth, behaving differently makes all the sense in the world.

The Bottom Line

Legalism occurs when we rip out the foundation of identity and try to get people to behave better. If you yank away the new heart message, you're left with nothing but a behavior improvement program—legalism. On the other hand, if you put the foundation of God's grace and our righteousness back in, you've got the Gospel.

Paul's letters usually affirm what God has done for us and to us first. Then, the latter chapters of his letters offer new ways to think and act because of who we are.

Our behavior flows from our identity, not vice versa.

CHAPTER 46

A few years ago, I received this encouraging note from Jasmin:

I just want to tell you what your ministry has done for me. For years, I felt like I couldn't say "no" to anyone when it came to doing things at church. Eventually, it got to the point where I was totally burned out and became resentful when people would ask me to do more.

Through understanding my righteousness in Christ, I've found freedom from people-pleasing. It's not that I don't do anything to serve now. I still do things, but it no longer feels like I'm filling a hole within me. I'm operating from the fullness or completeness in Christ that you talk about. I can say "yes" or "no" without feeling the pressure I once felt.

Thank you! I can say I know what it means to be led by the Spirit and to live from my heart.

More on Righteousness

Jasmin found that knowing her righteousness freed her from people-pleasing. "Righteousness." It's not a word we use in everyday conversation. It was a slang word back in the 1980s, as in "Ferris Bueller is one righteous dude." Other than this type of usage, the word seldom comes up.

Most believers know righteousness refers to right standing or rightness with God. But for centuries, religious scholars have debated whether the believer's righteousness is merely *imputed* (credited to us, like in a bank account) or actually *imparted* (literally shared or given to us by God).

Here's the truth: Both imputed and imparted righteousness are found in Scripture.

In Galatians 3 and Romans 4, we find righteousness was credited to Abraham by faith. By faith, we are offspring of Abraham. This means that righteousness has at least been credited to us. But we also have something better than Old Testament believers experienced (Hebrews 11:40). As we'll see, we have righteousness *imparted* to us by God.

In Galatians, we find our first clue that this is the case. The Law was not able to impart life to us. But Christ did impart life to us, and that's what gave us our righteousness. In short, we have an imparted-life type of righteousness.

*For if a law had been given that could **impart life**, then **righteousness** would certainly have come by the law.* (Galatians 3:21b)

Here, Paul equates life and righteousness. They're related, if not one and the same. We are righteous because we are alive in Christ. We became righteous when God imparted life to us. We have imparted life and an imparted-life righteousness. We are even called "the righteousness of God" (2 Corinthians 5:21).

It's amazing to me that we can believe we're born of God (1 John 5:1), born of the Spirit (John 3:6), and a partaker of the divine nature (2 Peter 1:4), yet still believe righteousness has not been imparted to us. What kind of person do we think God made us when He gave birth to us and brought us into His family? And given there's no mention of a future "nature change" in Heaven (only new bodies), what should we conclude about who we are now in this world?

> *If Christ is in you, though the body is dead because of sin,* **yet the spirit is alive because of righteousness.** (Romans 8:10)

> *He was delivered over to death for our sins and **was raised to life for our justification**.* (Romans 4:25)

Your spirit is alive because of righteousness. What does that tell you? You have a living righteousness, a life-giving righteousness. You are spiritually alive because of the righteousness that has been imparted to you (Romans 8:10).

How was it imparted? Through the resurrection. Jesus was raised from the dead to justify you, to make you righteous (Romans 4:25). God has given you a resurrection righteousness.

Righteousness Brings Release!

I received an email a few years ago from Jacob, who'd grown up in a strict Mennonite community. His family had lived apart from their neighbors; while they didn't drive horses and buggies, they did only drive black cars, the women wore dresses and small white head coverings, and there were many rules that governed their lives and their behavior.

> *My dad was a leader in our Mennonite community, and I grew up with a deep sense of how important morality and reputation in the community were. What I didn't realize at the time was how much I would be imposing that pressure on my kids later. So, when my eldest son got into drugs and ended up in jail, I nearly lost it. My emotions were out of control, and I said awful things and criticized him in ways that I now regret.*
>
> *Looking back, and with what I now know, I realize I was mostly worried about me and my own reputation. I blew up, because I was worried about what others would say about me (that I failed as a parent) and my family. I have asked my son for forgiveness, and we have come a long way since then.*
>
> *I want to thank you for your books as they helped me let my kids go from the expectations I held over them. I don't have to be "codependent," as they say, and can give myself permission to be okay (righteous!) regardless of my kids and what they are doing or are not doing. Ultimately, I cannot be responsible for all their choices, and*

I cannot live that way. I have found the stability I need in Christ, and for that I am grateful.

Do Nothing to Get More Righteous!

Who would see righteousness in Jesus as the cure for codependency? Most people might not, but Jacob did.

Righteousness means our children don't give us our identity. Righteousness means we can *release* our children (and others) and not derive our worth from them or their performance. The unshakeable righteousness we have in Jesus really is the answer to codependency.

After the first humans ate from the tree, God approached them and asked, "Who told you that you were naked?" (Genesis 3:11). God was asking them how they had arrived at the conclusion they were not okay. What standard had they adopted?

After eating from the tree, they decided to measure themselves in terms of good and evil, and they came up short. They didn't meet their own criteria. So they went away and hid in shame.

We do this too. We decide to measure ourselves based on our recent thoughts and feelings. We look at our performance to determine if we are okay. Inevitably, we conclude we're not: We're not righteous. We're not Christlike. Then we set out to be these things rather than believing, apart from our feelings, that we already are them.

God calls us to practice what I have called "the art of doing nothing"—nothing to get more forgiven, nothing to get more righteous, nothing to improve our status with Him.

This "art of doing nothing" is resting in the finished work of Christ.

The Bottom Line

Your slavery to sin was real. Your slavery to righteousness is just as real. God is *not* pretending you're righteous by looking at you with a pair of Jesus glasses on. You've got real righteousness. You've got resurrection righteousness.

Remember, anyone who is righteous at all is as righteous as Jesus. There's no middle ground. Nobody is 52 percent righteous. Nobody out there is "working on it." It's all or nothing. If you're righteous at all, you're "the righteousness of God" (2 Corinthians 5:21).

CHAPTER 47

When God looks at you, who does He see? This was the question Hannah had when she emailed me some time ago.

"My whole life, I was taught that when God looks at me, He sees Jesus. I never thought twice about it until recently," she wrote.

"It used to feel like a good thing, a comfort," Hannah continued, "but now I'm asking, 'Then how does God relate to me personally if He only sees Jesus instead?' In a way, it paints me as someone who is detestable to Him, so He must look away. If He were to see me for what I really look like, would He be disgusted? I know people aren't really saying that directly, but that's the feeling I get when I hear it."

Maybe you've heard that when God looks at you, He sees Jesus instead. If He were to look at you as you really are, it might make Him sick. So, He wears Jesus glasses in order to see you differently than you truly are.

People who believe this reveal they don't yet understand their new birth. Here's the truth: When God looks at you, He sees you! God doesn't need to look at Jesus instead of you. God looks right at you, and He likes what He sees. You are a fragrant aroma of Christ to God (2 Corinthians 2:15).

God can afford to look right at you because He took you through a radical heart surgery and changed who you are. He doesn't need to shield His eyes from you or look at you through a special Jesus filter.

God isn't tricking Himself. He's not pulling the wool over His own eyes. He's not pretending you're something you're not. No, God sees reality, and when He says you're righteous, He means it.

You really are righteous, so believe it and be happy.

"He Must Increase, but I Must Decrease"

I was sitting in the front row of a church I was visiting. I was one of the speakers at a multi-day conference being held there. I'd never been there before, and I didn't know most of the other pastors, so I wasn't sure what to expect.

"To increase the Kingdom, you must decrease!" the pastor who was speaking shouted. "You need to be less dominant and less prominent. Otherwise, God's glory is pushed down.

"It's all about Christ," he continued, "so step aside and make room for the King of kings. Live this principle of John the Baptist and watch God's Kingdom expand around you. More of Him, less of you!"

It was right after lunch, so I'd been fighting to pay attention—but at this, my eyes flew wide open. If I could have, I would've hit the pause button right there to shout back my response.

"Yes, we know John the Baptist said, 'He must increase; I must decrease,'" I would have said. "But John was saying his own ministry needed to phase out because Jesus was arriving on the scene with a new and better ministry. That had nothing to do with John the Baptist needing to diminish himself or get rid of himself. And it certainly isn't fuel for seeing yourself as an obstacle to God. You're not an obstacle to God. You're His instrument!"

I kept my cool and didn't say anything publicly. But hearing this taught reminded me yet again of why it's important to understand you're a new creation: so you can do away with believing the myth that you need to get out of God's way.

All of Him, None of You?

Maybe you've heard you need to "let go and let God" or that it needs to be "all of Him and none of you." That sounds super spiritual to say, but it still implies God is not okay with you in some way. Apparently, He needs to remove you from the situation. He needs to override you or circumvent you.

But is this the truth about who you are?

No, it doesn't need to be all of Him and none of you. It can be all of Him and all of you in a beautiful union together. You're compatible. He doesn't need to replace you; He already did that at the cross.

Now, He doesn't replace you. He embraces you.

We believers are the only ones who get to be ourselves and express Jesus at the same time. Now that's an incredible privilege!

God the Janitor?

Maybe you've heard God is like a janitor, progressively going through your house and cleaning everything up. Room by room, your heart starts to belong to Him more and more. Let's just hope He doesn't see what's in the closet!

While this makes for an interesting sermon analogy, the truth is that God owns all of you. You're a person of God's possession (1 Peter 2:9). You've been sealed with the Holy Spirit, and every bit of you belongs to God (1 Corinthians 6:19–20).

God has taken up residence inside of you and called you "home." Sure, there may be some trash in the yard (old attitudes and actions) that He's still working on in your life. But you, as the house of God, are complete in Christ. You belong fully to Him.

Have you noticed the Bible doesn't speak of any future change to you in Heaven except for your body? You're told you'll get a new resurrection body, but other than that, it appears *you're Heaven-ready*. This means your spirit and your soul are ready to go to Heaven at any moment, without any last-minute cleanup job.

This is incredible to ponder: There's nothing intrinsically wrong with who you are. Yes, you experience the presence of influencers—the flesh and the power of sin. But you are not those. You are a child of God, accepted in the Beloved (Ephesians 1:6).

PART 6

CLOSER THAN YOU IMAGINE!

CHAPTER 48

This chapter isn't about a question I've gotten many times over the years.

It's about a question I almost never hear.

That's right—after nearly two decades of hosting live call-in radio programs addressing thousands of questions, after teaching sermons and conference sessions at churches and events across North America, there's one important question hardly anyone asks: *What does it mean to have Christ living in me and to be complete in Him?*

Don't get me wrong—I've heard hundreds of questions about salvation. Often, I ask those callers point-blank: "Does Jesus Christ live in you?" and the responses I get are fascinating. "I grew up in a Christian home," they'll say, or "I go to church." Some will say "I've been baptized," or "I'm a member

of such-and-such congregation." (The only answer that satisfies me is: "Yes, I know that Jesus Christ lives in me.")

That's not what I'm talking about here. I'm not talking
about inviting Christ to live in you. I'm talking about what it
means to have Him living in you today. I find it fascinating
and shocking that hardly anyone asks about whether Christ
lives through them and how His indwelling presence affects
their everyday perspective and life.

Almost nobody's talking about it at all. I've asked myself
why many times, and I think it comes down to this: Most of
us are still asking questions about Friday, so to speak. We just
haven't graduated to Sunday. In other words, most of us are
still asking "cross" questions:

Am I forgiven of the sins that plague me?
Does God really accept me as I am?
Did I do something to mess up my relationship with God?

If you don't have solid answers to these cross questions,
it's hard to move on to get your resurrection questions
answered. I'm talking about questions such as:

What does it mean that Christ lives in me?
How do I live from my union with Jesus?
What should I expect from His indwelling life?

If you've made it this far in the book, and you've been paying attention to how amazing it is to be totally forgiven and to
live under grace as a new creation, then maybe it's time we now
focus on what it means to have life—His resurrection life.

Eternal Life Is Christ's Life

Eternal life is more than everlasting life. Eternal life is not your life made longer. Eternal life is not your life made better. Eternal life is actually Christ's life.

The word "eternal" means "having no beginning and no end." Whose life is the only life with no beginning? God's life, of course. To have eternal life is to have the life of God within you through the person of Jesus Christ.

> *And this is the testimony:* **God has given us eternal life, and this life is in his Son. Whoever has the Son has life;** *whoever does not have the Son of God does not have life. I write these things to you who believe in the name of the Son of God so that you may know that you have eternal life.* (1 John 5:11–13)

Eternal life isn't just a ticket to Heaven. Having eternal life is not primarily about reading a book or visiting a building for an hour a week. Whoever has the Son has the life. Having eternal life means having the Son's life. The life lost in Eden is restored in Christ.

A building of brick and mortar is not the house of God. You are!

More than Book Knowledge

Some may think experiencing eternal life is about book knowledge—knowing facts and figures from the Bible. Jesus Himself dismissed that idea:

*You study the Scriptures diligently because you think that in them you have eternal life. **These are the very Scriptures that testify about me, yet you refuse to come to me to have life.*** (John 5:39–40)

The Jews were certainly dedicated to studying Scripture and memorizing what it said. But getting to know the book is way different from getting to know the Author. You can see how easy it is to get off track.

I taught linguistics for two decades and wrote a textbook. My students read the textbook to get to know linguistics, not to get to know me. Growing up in school, you read your math book to learn the formulas. You read your history book to learn the facts. Likely, you never once thought about getting to know the author of those textbooks. But the Bible really is different. It's ultimately not about being an expert in the Book. It's about knowing the Author.

Now this is eternal life: that they know you, the only true God, and Jesus Christ, whom you have sent. (John 17:3)

The Test: Is Christ in You?

The presence of Christ Himself within us is nothing short of miraculous. It's the core of true Christianity. Paul says the test you need to pass is this:

Test yourselves *to see if you are in the faith; examine yourselves! Or do you not recognize this about yourselves,* *that Jesus Christ is in you—unless indeed you fail the test?* (2 Corinthians 13:5)

The best revelation a Christian can have is that you possess all of Jesus Christ all of the time. You contain within you every attribute of Christ at every moment.

Need more patience? Don't wait for a gift package to fall from Heaven. Trust Christ within you here and now. Need more love? Recognize God poured out His love into your heart through His Spirit (Romans 5:5). You have all you need.

There's no more waiting or hoping or begging or pleading. Instead, count yourself alive and connected to the One Who is pure patience and pure love. No more long-distance phone calls to Heaven asking for a special visit of God's Spirit to "help." The presence of Christ is local, powerful, and all-encompassing. He is everything you need!

*And my God will meet **all your needs** according to the riches of his glory **in Christ Jesus**.* (Philippians 4:19)

Complete in Him

Our union with the resurrected Christ means our attempts at getting "more of Jesus" can come to a screeching halt. We're complete in Him.

*For in Christ all the fullness of the Deity lives in bodily form, and **in Christ you have been brought to full-ness**. He is the head over every power and authority.* (Colossians 2:9–10)

If you've spent any time in the Christian world, I'm sure you've heard something like this: "It's great you're a Christian, but now you need the Spirit" or "It's great you're a believer, but now you need this spiritual gift."

Peter tells us if we're in Christ, we don't need anything else:

> *His divine power has given us everything we need for a godly life* through our knowledge of him who called us by his own glory and goodness. (2 Peter 1:3)

Could we have everything we need for a godly life yet be lacking God's Spirit? Impossible!

God blessed us with every spiritual blessing in Christ Jesus (Ephesians 1:3). This includes all of the Holy Spirit we'll ever need. No one has salvation and then gets God's Spirit later. They're one and the same. He who has the Son has the life (1 John 5:12).

The Bottom Line

Are we supposed to hunger and thirst for more of God?

Actually, it's the opposite. Jesus said, "I am the bread of life. Whoever comes to me will never go hungry, and whoever believes in me will never be thirsty" (John 6:35). The entirety of Christ Himself is joined to you, twenty-four hours a day, seven days a week, without interruption.

Why would we hunger and thirst for more of God when we have all of Him through the indwelling of Jesus? Next time you hear that you need to hunger and thirst for more of

God, hit the pause button. Recognize while that sounds very religious, it's just not the truth of the Gospel.

You've been blessed with every spiritual blessing (Ephesians 1:3). And you have everything you need for life and godliness (2 Peter 1:3). No more hungering and no more thirsting.

Instead, celebrate all you have in Jesus!

CHAPTER 49

One night, Tyrone from Louisiana called in to our radio program with a question about closeness to God. Like so many people, he just didn't feel close all the time, and that discouraged him.

"I want to know how I can get closer to God," he began. "I want to be more like Him and stay close to Him. I want to give Him all my problems and my heartache. I am getting ready to go back into the hospital for another surgery on my heart, and I need to know this. I've tried so hard, but I still worry. I don't sleep. I don't rest. I feel depressed. I just don't know what to do. I want to get really close to Him and to serve Him and be a good disciple for Him, but I don't know how."

Tyrone's sincerity was evident, and his circumstances sounded overwhelming. Anyone would feel worried and depressed with serious heart problems; but what seemed to be bothering him the most was the feeling that God wasn't close to him.

"Tyrone, I have good news for you," I began. "Did you know that Jesus Christ has become your life and Jesus Christ is one spirit with you? Romans 6 says you were united with Christ in His death, burial, and resurrection.

"So, I want you to imagine yourself right now," I continued, "enveloped in Christ, inserted in Christ right now. You are in Christ, and Christ is in you. You are as close as you can get to Christ. You're one spirit with Him.

"That's the truth," I told him, "but in the meantime you've got all these emotions. You've got physical difficulties, and you're going into the hospital. You're going to undergo another surgery, and your emotions can be overloaded with fear. Your thoughts may be, 'God, I feel dirty' or 'God, I feel distant' or 'Where are you, God?'

"My prayer for you is that you would see where you already are. I want you to see that you're as close as you can get. I want you to see that you're in the arms of your God and seated at God's right hand in heavenly places, in Christ. This is what the Gospel teaches."

I could have imitated a lot of religious teachers by telling Tyrone that if he just read his Bible more, then he would feel closer. Or if he just attended church more or shared Christ more, then he'd feel closer. But it's just not true. That's not why we are close to God.

You are close to God through the death and the resurrection of Jesus alone. You are close to God through what Jesus did for you, not what you're doing for Him. You could never do enough. You could never get close enough. So God made you one spirit with Christ (1 Corinthians 6:17). You can't get any closer than one spirit with the Lord.

As Close as You'll Ever Get!

Tyrone is not the only one. It seems like believers today have adopted the idea of inching closer to God through Bible study and what we've called "spiritual disciplines." But that's not how the New Testament speaks of your closeness to God. Consider this:

- You're one spirit with the Lord (1 Corinthians 6:17).
- You're united with Christ (Romans 6:5).
- Christ literally and actually lives inside of you (Colossians 1:27).
- You can't get closer than the Vine-branches relationship you already enjoy (John 15:5).

This means you can stop the restless activity of trying to get close and stay close to God. *You are as close to God as you'll ever get.*

This is the closeness Jesus prayed for. He prayed "that all of them may be one, Father, just as you are in me and I am in you. May they also be in us" (John 17:21a). Jesus asked the Father for us to be bonded and fused together with Him. His prayer was answered!

I have been crucified with Christ and I no longer live, but Christ lives in me. The life I now live in the body, I

*live by faith in the Son of God, who loved me and gave
himself for me.* (Galatians 2:20)

You now live but as a new creation in Christ. And Christ
lives in you. That's as close to Jesus as a person can be: You're
compatible and connected to Him.

Your closeness with God is not a feeling. You've been
brought near by the blood of Jesus (Ephesians 2:13), and you've
been united to Christ through the resurrection. You live every
day in this closeness, whether you feel it or not.

You do learn and grow in your understanding, but this
doesn't change your proximity to Christ. You have a permanent oneness with Him as a free gift from God. Your union
with Jesus is not something you sustain. It's something God
achieved for you and freely gifted to you.

Perfect closeness to God is absolutely free. You'll never be
dirty or distant again. Count yourself clean and close, today
and every day.

A Mystery Now Revealed

"Christ in you" was a mystery kept hidden for ages but is
now revealed to us:

> *To them God has chosen to make known among the
> Gentiles the glorious riches of **this mystery, which is
> Christ in you**, the hope of glory.* (Colossians 1:27)

Jesus proclaimed, "I am the resurrection and the life"
(John 11:25). He announced Himself as the way and the

truth and the life (John 14:6). He said, "Because I live, you also will live" (John 14:19).

The cross brought you total forgiveness. The cross brought you freedom from the Law. The cross brought your old self to an end. But without the resurrection, you would be lying in a spiritual tomb. You would have no existence.

> *For if, while we were God's enemies, we were **reconciled to him through the death** of his Son, how much more, having been reconciled, shall we be **saved through his life**!* (Romans 5:10)

The resurrection of Christ actually saves you. Without the resurrection, you'd still be dead in your sins:

> *And if Christ has not been raised, our preaching is **useless** and so is your faith.... And if Christ has not been raised, your faith is futile; **you are still in your sins**.* (1 Corinthians 15:14, 17)

The resurrection is the centerpiece of the Christian faith. Without it, there's no salvation. Without it, we don't have new life in Jesus. If there's no resurrection life in us, then everything about Christianity is a waste of time.

Salvation isn't you giving your life to Christ. It's Christ's giving His life to you. Sure, you offered your life to God at salvation. But He crucified your old life and gave you a new one. It's His resurrection life that saved you.

You're forgiven by Christ's death and saved by His life!

The Resurrected Teacher Within

There are loads of religious movements that follow the teachings of a dead teacher. What separates us from those religions is our Teacher is alive today and living in us. We're not simply looking back to the four gospels and imitating the actions of a historical figure. No, we're being led internally by the resurrected Christ Himself. Instead of asking WWJD ("What Would Jesus Do?"), we can ask, "What is Christ doing in me today?"

Many describe their relationship with Christ as "following" Him. They call themselves "followers of Jesus." While there's nothing wrong with this, it doesn't tell the whole story. Following doesn't capture the big picture that you're being led internally. Your new self is bonded to Christ. You're not merely imitating the actions of Jesus from recorded history. The Teacher is alive, living in you, and you're inspired from within.

Never Lost in the Process

You're not lost in the process. You don't function as a Jesus firehose—only meant to give Him away to others. Christ is not like a flow of energy through an electrical cable. He's a Person, and you're in relationship with Him. He wants you involved all the way. *You're not a hollow tube. You're a child of God!*

God has invited you to both trust Him and be yourself. Remember, you can be yourself and express Jesus at the same time, with no conflict.

In the Old Testament, there's the story of the burning bush. It says the angel of the Lord was present in the bush, but the fire didn't consume it (Exodus 3:2). This is a beautiful picture to me of what it means to have Christ living in you without consuming you. The supernatural dwells within the natural but does not burn it up.

You're the creation, and you're designed to be inhabited by the Creator. You're a perfect fit. This was God's intention from the beginning.

The Bottom Line

You're called to recognize the presence of the Teacher within as you go about your day, being yourself and enjoying Him. You are as close to Jesus as you can possibly be. Perfect closeness to God was freely given to you by grace.

In this perfect bond you enjoy, God isn't seeking to diminish you in the slightest. He created you, pursued you, saved you, and indwelt you for a reason. You're invited to participate along with Him in a beautiful union.

There's nothing else like it!

CHAPTER 50

I receive a lot of questions about finding and staying in God's will. Often, people grow up in the church. They're taught God has a plan for their life. They seek after it; they may have other people tell them what "the plan" is. But eventually, life just doesn't satisfy, and they start to wonder: Did I miss something God was telling me? Am I now out of His will? How do I get back in?

An email I received from Lisa embodies this fear:

I grew up in a Christian home, and I went to a Christian school all my life. I dedicated my life to the Lord at a young age. I sought His will to the best of my knowledge, but somewhere along the way I must have made a mistake and married the wrong person. I'm now in a marriage that is practically dead. It feels like my husband and I are just roommates. He works all the time and barely talks to me and the kids. I was so sure when we got married that this was God's will for both of us. Where did I go wrong?

Circumstances turn bad, and people around us make harmful choices. Then we wonder how we got in the situation in the first place if we were faithfully "seeking God's will."

Seeking God's Will

How many of us have been perplexed about God's will? We freeze up like a deer in the headlights, wondering if we've missed His will and how we can get back in.

Is this what God intended for us—the paralysis of analysis?

I grew up hearing God's *perfect* will is like the center of a bullseye. And just outside of the bullseye is His *permissive* will. If you miss that, I guess you're in the "outer ring of darkness." There's no coming back from there!

How do you supposedly "stay" in God's perfect will? By listening really hard to everything He wants you to choose. And if you can't hear anything, it could be because there are unconfessed sins stopping up your ears.

Can you see how paralyzing this view of God's will is?

Which car? Which house? Which spouse? We go through life's decisions, waiting to hear from God about every little thing. Sometimes, all we hear are crickets—nothing. And we say, "God, where are you?"

Meanwhile, a quick study of God's will in the Bible reveals there's no mystery to it. God's will is that salvation be presented to everyone (Ephesians 1:5–2:22). God's will is that none perish and all believe (2 Peter 3:9; 1 Timothy 2:4). God's will is that we give thanks for Jesus and communicate transparently with our Father (1 Thessalonians 5:16–18). God's will is that we wake up every day and present our bodies to Him (Romans 12:1–2). Finally, God's will is that we bear the fruit of the Spirit (Colossians 1:9–12; John 15:8).

Here's the plain truth: God's will is Jesus. You're always in Him, so don't worry about falling out. You don't have to stress. God is behind every door, because when you walk through it, Christ is in you!

Yes, we ask God for wisdom (James 1:5). But God's will is that we express Christ in every moment. It's that simple. It's not about choosing the perfect house and the perfect spouse and the perfect car. While it might seem really spiritual to ask God to pick all these things for us, it's not really what God wants for us. It results in immaturity as we're led around by impulses rather than seeking to make wise decisions and learning from our choices.

In fact, it's works-based righteousness. Think about it: What do you call it when someone believes they're keeping themselves "in" God's will (in right standing with God) through the daily decisions they make?

That's works-based righteousness!

Let's recognize God's will is Jesus Christ. Since you're in Him, you're always in God's will. You'll never fall out. He'll never leave you (Hebrews 13:5), and no one can snatch you away from Him (John 10:28). This freedom means you can do what God desires (and what you really want!) without wondering if you're in the right place or making all the right choices.

Abiding in Christ

Jim from Arkansas wrote me a three-page letter sharing his journey out of legalism. He still wasn't quite free, so he had some questions.

"I spent nearly two decades under 'victorious life' type teaching," he began. "There was a deep emphasis on needing to 'abide in Christ', but how to do it was never really explained.

"As a result, there seemed to be two groups of people in our church," he continued. "There were the ones who just 'got it' and the ones who didn't. I never felt like I really knew what it was to abide. Years later, I'm still trying to figure it out, and I'm confused about the whole thing. Can you help?"

What a tragedy. Imagine spending years, even decades, trying to grasp for something that is never quite within reach. Or maybe you don't have to imagine it. Maybe you've lived it!

Over the years, I've heard many sermons about how we need to try to abide, seek to abide, and work to abide in Christ. But understanding our union with Christ can help us see "abiding in Christ" in a new light.

You see, when you realize you're in Christ and He is in you, all that mental effort comes to an end. The word "abide" just means "to live." I abide in Texas. I make my abode there. I don't have to try to abide in Texas. It's just a fact. It's my location. Likewise, if you're a believer, then you do abide in Christ. You live in Him. It's just a fact.

When Jesus spoke of abiding in Him, He was contrasting unbelievers with believers. This is why He said apart from Him you could do nothing. But as a believer, you're never apart from Him. You're always abiding in Him. You always live in Him (Romans 8:9). This is why Jesus said any branch that doesn't abide in Him is burned. Believers won't be burned. Why not? Because we do abide (live) in Him.

So, you don't need to turn "abiding" into some sort of work you maintain or sustain. Instead, you can count yourself alive to God. You're *already* in a Vine-branches relationship with Jesus and always abiding in Him.

Put God First?

For you, maybe the struggle was never as much about "finding God's will" or "abiding" as it was "putting God first." You've probably heard you need to put Him first in your life, and it sounded so spiritual.

I believe the Gospel reveals something much more meaningful: You don't have to put God first. Christ is your life. Christ is not merely a part of your life. He is your life!

God is not competing with your family, your job, your hobbies, or your interests. Colossians 3 says that Christ is your life (Colossians 3:4). Paul says that, to him, to live is Christ (Philippians 1:21). Paul isn't prioritizing things in his life to "get God first."

Paul is recognizing something deeper. He's saying whether we engage in activities with family, or at work, or in our hobbies, Christ is our life in all things. He's not competing with them. He's inspiring us in the midst of them.

Give God More Glory?

Maybe you've heard you need to make sure to give God all the glory. I've seen people literally refuse compliments and dance around their obvious involvement in an effort to "give

God all the glory." Here's a news flash: God already has all the glory He needs. In fact, God doesn't need us to give Him anything.

> *And he is not served by human hands, as if he needed* *anything.* *Rather, he himself gives everyone life and breath and everything else.* (Acts 17:25)

Not only does God not need anything from us, He decided to give us more than we could ever ask for or imagine. God even shared His glory with us!

> *I have given them the glory that you gave me,* *that they may be one as we are one.* (John 17:22)

What if all the time and energy you've spent trying to stay in God's will, abide in Him, put Him first, and give Him the glory could be spent another way?

Imagine. Well, you don't have to imagine if you make it a reality. Go ahead, believe the truth, be set free, and spend more time thanking God and loving others.

CHAPTER 51

Charlie called in to our nightly radio program from Nevada to ask another common question. It relates to "surrendering" to God. Here's how he put it:

"I've been saved since I was as a teenager, but ever since, I've struggled with obsessive-compulsive thinking," he shared. "Some people call it my 'doubting disease,' and I'm going through counseling right now.

"I've been told what I'm lacking is total surrender to God. At times in my life I think I've done it, but then I ask myself: Would I be willing to drop anything? Would I do anything for God? And sometimes, truthfully the answer is *no*. But if I'm truly a believer, shouldn't the answer be *yes*? That's why I doubt I'm actually saved."

I thanked Charlie for trusting us with his question. It's hard to call into a live radio program and share something you've been struggling with. Then I re-phrased his problem: "What you're really asking, my friend, is: Am I brave enough? Would I leave behind anything and everything at a moment's notice? Am I committed and dedicated enough to the Lord?"

"That's right," he agreed, "and often I feel the answer is *no*."

"Here's the good news, then," I said. "You're not saved by your bravery. No one is saved by their bravery. You're saved by the bravery of Jesus Christ on that cross. He was obedient even unto death. You're saved by His bravery, not yours."

Charlie was experiencing accusation from the enemy regarding his salvation. That accusation sounds like: "Are you sure you would do anything for God? Because if you're not absolutely sure you would do anything for Him, you're probably not really saved." That's how the deceiver sows seeds of doubt. That's exactly what seemed to be happening in Charlie.

I also pointed out that the word "surrender" sounds super spiritual and humble yet never appears in the New Testament to describe our relationship with God. The reality is that with most people, the word evokes a military battle. We think of giving in to an opposing army. So, when somebody tells us we need to surrender to God, we immediately think of God being like an opposing army conquering us. We must give up and give in to Him and surrender.

"However, the truth of the Gospel is you're in God's family and you're on God's team," I concluded. "The biblical expression for what you do with God is you 'offer' or 'present' your body to Him. Romans says your body is holy and acceptable to God."

Presenting your body to God is not about getting saved. It's about bearing fruit: "Lord Jesus Christ, I'm going to trust

You today. I present my body to You, and I want You to express Yourself through me so I can experience true fulfillment. I want You to love people through me today. I'm excited about what You're going to do in my life today."

Think of a seven-year-old who receives Jesus as their Savior, I told Charlie. They're not trying to win a bravery contest. They just know they need Jesus. They want Him in their life. They believe He rose from the dead, and they open their heart to Him. They're not thinking, "I need to be brave enough. I need to be committed enough. I need to be sold out enough." That's not how we're saved.

"How about the person who is paralyzed in a hospital bed?" I then asked. "They received Christ, yet they cannot prove their dedication to Him in an outward way on the mission field or by going door-to-door sharing Christ. But it's not about their bravery, either. They're trusting in the bravery of Jesus Christ, who was obedient to the point of death. It's all about Him."

Finally, I told Charlie, "Any message focused on how 'surrendered' you are is honestly a fleshly, religious message." I wasn't surprised he was hearing it. It's very easy for someone to stand up on Sunday morning and tell everyone they need to be sold out, to give up everything, or else they may not be saved in the first place.

"You're just not brave enough" is a very easy sermon to prepare, but it ignores the finished work of Christ. You'll recognize a message like that because it comes off like a high school pep rally or a *Braveheart* speech with the goal of making you feel horrible about your level of commitment. It's often accompanied by a bulleted list of things you've made into "idols"—your job, your hobbies, even your family. It makes God look desperate to compete with these, and it's all your fault for not putting Him ahead of everything else on the list.

Surrender?

We often hear the term "surrender"—the idea that we need to give up and give in to God. But does the New Testament actually describe our role in this way? Not once are believers told to "surrender" to God. We're never cast as being on a different team from God.

As I shared with Charlie, the term "surrender" in everyday speech is typically used to describe the action of giving up and giving in to an enemy army. Picture the white flag being raised and waved as you throw up your hands and announce you've been beaten into submission.

Is this what God asks? Is this how He treats you?

No, you're not called to surrender, because you're already on God's team and in His family. Instead, you simply offer your body to Him every day (Romans 12:1). Why? Because if Christ is your life, it makes sense to offer your body to Him. God has the market cornered on fulfillment, and nothing else satisfies you anyway.

Maybe you've heard God is trying to get you out of your comfort zone. This sounds really spiritual, but the truth is the opposite. The Holy Spirit is your Comforter and your Counselor. Apparently, He wants you in a zone of comfort with Him. God is working in you to *do* His good pleasure. But it's more than that—He's working in you to *desire* what He wants, too.

*For it is God who is at work in you, **both to desire and to work** for His good pleasure.* (Philippians 2:13 NASB)

God isn't asking you to do something you don't really want to do. First, He puts it on your heart (you want it!). Second, He's leading you into it. The bottom line is that you don't have to be scared to offer your body to God. The Lord is good, and what He has for you is good. His plan is always a perfect fit with who you are.

What about Growth?

I know you want to grow quickly. But I would ask you: Why? Most people's answer boils down to wanting to perform better. But what if God is not in a hurry with you?

Did you know even Jesus grew in wisdom and stature (Luke 2:52)? Yet He wasn't becoming more righteous. He was righteous the whole time. Apparently, we're free to grow in our understanding and watch our performance change, but we're "the righteousness of God" (2 Corinthians 5:21) along the way.

That means the pressure is off.

You really can trust the growth "from God" (Colossians 2:19). Our growth is God's problem, and He's always right on time.

You may be thinking: "But God says, 'continue to work out your salvation with fear and trembling' (Philippians 2:12), so how can you be so relaxed about growth?"

We can be confident and restful about our growth in Christ. God began a beautiful work in us, and He will continue it

(Philippians 1:6). We work out our salvation. We don't work for it. We work out what God has already worked in!

The Bottom Line

Your union with Christ has radical implications for how you live the Christian life. You can wake up every day and live the same way you got started in Jesus:

> *So then, **just as you received Christ Jesus as Lord, continue to live your lives in him, rooted and built up in him**, strengthened in the faith as you were taught, and overflowing with thankfulness.* (Colossians 2:6–7)

How did you start with Jesus? You began by admitting you couldn't save yourself and only He could. So now, wake up every day and admit you can't live the Christian life without Jesus. Apart from Him, you can do nothing. But thank God you're never apart from Jesus, and your union with Him can be the source of all you do.

CHAPTER 52

Another question people often ask is about being filled with the Spirit. How does it happen, and what does it mean? Tracey put it this way in an email to me:

> I heard a preacher the other day saying we need to be constantly filled with the Spirit. On the other hand, though, I've heard you say we have all of the Holy Spirit we'll ever need.
>
> I believe you, as you shared all the Scriptures that show we believers are fully equipped. But there are still passages in Acts where it talks about individual believers who are "full of the Spirit." Why would it use that language if we all have the Spirit? I'm talking about passages like these:

Brothers and sisters, **choose seven men from among you who are known to be full of the Spirit** and wisdom. We will turn this responsibility over to them. (Acts 6:3)

[Barnabas] was **a good man, full of the Holy Spirit** and faith, and a great number of people were brought to the Lord. (Acts 11:24)

Can you help me put these in context so I can understand "filled with the Spirit" better?

Tracey knew the truth, but she was struggling to reconcile what she'd heard with what the Bible itself says.

More of the Spirit?

"First," I told her, "being filled with the Spirit is indeed something ongoing."

The verbiage Paul uses in Ephesians 5:18 is "be filled" (present imperative). But it doesn't mean getting more of God's Spirit. You're not reaching outside of yourself to get more of Him to come in. That already occurred at salvation. You were sealed once and for all with the Holy Spirit until the day of redemption. You have everything you need for life and godliness, and that certainly includes having God's Spirit.

You're complete in Him. You're in the Spirit, and the Spirit is in you. When Paul says not to be drunk with wine but to be filled with the Spirit (Ephesians 5:18), what does he mean? If we can't get more of the Spirit, then what does "be filled" mean?

Consider this: Why do people look to too much wine? They're looking for relaxation. They're looking for a sense of peace and calm. That's what wine does for a person: It calms them. That's also—not coincidentally—what love does for a person.

Just two chapters earlier in Ephesians, Paul says if we get to know how gigantic God's love is for us, we will be filled to the measure of the fullness of God.

> ... *to grasp how wide and long and high and deep is the love of Christ, and to know this love that surpasses knowledge—that you may be filled to the measure of all the fullness of God.* (Ephesians 3:18b–19)

To be "filled with the Spirit" is to be inspired by the love of Jesus. Now it all comes together. What does God's love do for you? Similar to wine, it relaxes you and gives you a sense of peace and calm. Paul is saying, "Don't be dependent on alcohol for your peace. Let yourself be inspired and motivated and relaxed and calmed by the love of Christ."

Filled with the Spirit

Being filled with the Spirit doesn't mean getting more of God's Spirit to come live in you. He already lives within you.

Think of a two-liter bottle of soda. You put the cap on it and screw it tight, and then you start shaking it. What happens? It starts fizzing up inside. The bottle is already filled and sealed. It's not getting any more soda inside it. But once you start shaking it, there's new activity happening on the inside. Likewise, we have all of the Spirit we'll ever need living inside us. But we certainly aren't always motivated by God's love. We're learning about God's great love for us every day, and there's new agape-inspired activity fizzing up on the inside.

When Paul says in Acts to choose men who are "full of the Spirit", he's saying choose people inspired and motivated by God's love. If they're going to be waiting on tables, they need to be hospitable and loving as they serve food and drink. If they represent the Body of Christ, they need to be people who know and express the gigantic love of Jesus.

Maybe certain flavors of Christianity have tainted the idea of being "filled with the Spirit" for you. But a quick look through Acts reveals being "full of the Spirit" is a description of the believer's motivation—with a variety of actions taken. For example, "filled with the Spirit" describes the apostles' motivation as they shared or defended the Gospel, or experienced joy in the midst of persecution (Acts 2:4; 4:8, 31; 6:3; 7:55; 11:24; 13:9, 52). God's great love motivates all these actions and any action taken in dependency on Him.

Being filled with the Spirit is compatible with every aspect of our lives, even when we show hospitality or encounter trouble. And why wouldn't it be? Being motivated by the enormous love of Jesus Christ intersects with every moment of our day and all we do.

God Is Love

Is God kind and friendly to you? Or is that just a Walt Disney view of Him? Is He supportive and encouraging and always on your side? Maybe you believe that's just a feel-good message, too good to be true?

But remember, God is love (1 John 4:8). And what does perfect love look like?

> *Love is **patient**, love is **kind**. It does not envy, it does not boast, it is not proud. It does not dishonor others, it is **not self-seeking**, it is **not easily angered**, it keeps **no record of wrongs**. Love does not delight in evil but rejoices with the truth. **It always protects, always trusts, always hopes, always perseveres.*** (1 Corinthians 13:4–8)

We typically hear this passage at weddings, as we sit in the audience with our eyes on the bride and groom. If we've been married a decade or two, we might be thinking, "Good luck with all that." If we're on the younger side, we might start taking mental notes, "Now I've got my to-do list for guaranteed success in marriage!"

But Paul's treatise on God's love is not an activities checklist. It's a description of love, and therefore a description of God. This is the kind of love you "possess" (1 Corinthians 13:1–3) within you in the person of Jesus. It's also the treatment you can expect from God.

God is patient with you. God is kind to you. God is not rude to you. God keeps no record of your wrongs. God always trusts you. God never fails you.

The Bottom Line

You are deeply loved, completely forgiven, and never alone. As you come to know the love of Christ more, God's love will overflow to other people.

Nothing delights your Father more than when you relax in His outrageous love for you. People can't see the invisible God, but you are a visible reflection of His invisible love.

Knowing the gigantic love of Christ—that's what being filled with the Spirit is all about. That's what the grace message is all about.

That's what life itself is all about!

THE GRACE MESSAGE: A SCRIPTURE GUIDE

I've been given the right to be a child of God.	Jn. 1:12
I'm born again and can see the kingdom of God.	Jn. 3:3
I will not perish, and I have eternal life.	Jn. 3:16
I believe in Jesus, and I am not judged.	Jn. 3:18
I don't need to thirst for more of Jesus.	Jn. 4:14
I worship the Father in spirit and in truth.	Jn. 4:23–24
I will not come into judgment.	Jn. 5:24
I have passed out of death into life.	Jn. 5:24
I don't need to hunger or thirst for more.	Jn. 6:35
Jesus will never cast me out.	Jn. 6:37
Jesus will raise me up on the last day.	Jn. 6:40
From my inner being flows rivers of living water.	Jn. 7:38
I have the Light of life.	Jn. 8:12
I know the truth, and it makes me free.	Jn. 8:32
Jesus has made me free indeed.	Jn. 8:36
Jesus knows me, and I know Him.	Jn. 10:14
I know Jesus, and I follow His voice.	Jn. 10:27

No one will snatch me out of Jesus's hand.	Jn. 10:28
Jesus is my resurrection life. I will never die.	Jn. 11:25–26
I have become a child of light.	Jn. 12:36
The Helper will be with me forever.	Jn. 14:16
I am in Christ, and Christ is in me.	Jn. 14:20
The Holy Spirit will teach me all things.	Jn. 14:26
I am a branch abiding in the Vine (Jesus).	Jn. 15:5
I am a friend of Jesus.	Jn. 15:15
The Holy Spirit discloses the things of Jesus to me.	Jn. 16:14
I am not of this world.	Jn. 17:16
I am in the Father and in the Son.	Jn. 17:21
I have received Christ's glory.	Jn. 17:22
God's love is in me.	Jn. 17:26
I have been baptized with the Holy Spirit.	Acts 1:5
I am Jesus's witness.	Acts 1:8
I called on the name of the Lord and was saved.	Acts 2:21
I received the gift of the Holy Spirit.	Acts 2:38
I believed, and I received forgiveness of sins.	Acts 10:43
I have turned from darkness to light.	Acts 26:18
I have received forgiveness and an inheritance.	Acts 26:18
I have been sanctified by faith in Jesus.	Acts 26:18
My sins are not taken into account.	Rom. 4:8
I have peace with God.	Rom. 5:1
The love of God was poured into my heart.	Rom. 5:5
I am saved from wrath through Jesus.	Rom. 5:9
I have been saved by Christ's life.	Rom. 5:10
I received an abundance of grace.	Rom. 5:17
I received the gift of righteousness.	Rom. 5:17
I reign in life through Jesus Christ.	Rom. 5:17
I have been made righteous.	Rom. 5:19
I have died to sin.	Rom. 6:2
I was crucified and buried with Christ.	Rom. 6:3–4
I was raised to newness of life in Him.	Rom. 6:4–5

My old self was crucified with Him.	Rom. 6:6
I died and was freed from sin.	Rom. 6:7
I am dead to sin and alive to God.	Rom. 6:10–11
I am not under law but under grace.	Rom. 6:14
I became obedient from the heart.	Rom. 6:17
I am a slave of righteousness.	Rom. 6:18
I have been freed from sin.	Rom. 6:22
I died to the Law.	Rom. 7:4
I have been joined to Jesus.	Rom. 7:4
I serve in the newness of the Spirit.	Rom. 7:6
There is now no condemnation for me.	Rom. 8:1
I've been set free from sin and death.	Rom. 8:2
The Law has been fulfilled in me.	Rom. 8:4
I can now walk by the Spirit.	Rom. 8:5
I can now set my mind on the Spirit.	Rom. 8:6
I am not in the flesh but in the Spirit.	Rom. 8:9
My spirit is alive because of righteousness.	Rom. 8:10
The Spirit of God lives in me.	Rom. 8:11
I am a child of God led by His Spirit.	Rom. 8:14
God is my "Daddy Father."	Rom. 8:15
God's Spirit testifies with my spirit.	Rom. 8:16
I am a fellow heir with Christ.	Rom. 8:17
My body is a living and holy sacrifice.	Rom. 12:1
God is renewing my mind.	Rom. 12:2
I have been sanctified in Christ.	1 Cor. 1:2
God called me into fellowship with Jesus.	1 Cor. 1:9
By God's doing, I am in Christ Jesus.	1 Cor. 1:30
I have the mind of Christ.	1 Cor. 2:16
I am a temple of God.	1 Cor. 3:16
I belong to Christ.	1 Cor. 3:23
I will judge the world and the angels.	1 Cor. 6:2–3
I was washed, sanctified, and justified.	1 Cor. 6:11
My body is a member of Christ.	1 Cor. 6:15, 19

I am one spirit with the Lord.	1 Cor. 6:17
I have been bought with a price.	1 Cor. 6:20
I love God, and I am known by Him.	1 Cor. 8:3
I am gifted exactly as God wants me to be.	1 Cor. 12:11
God comforts me in all my affliction.	2 Cor. 1:4
God placed His Spirit in my heart.	2 Cor. 1:22
I am a fragrance of Christ to God.	2 Cor. 2:15
My adequacy is from God.	2 Cor. 3:5
I am a minister of the new covenant.	2 Cor. 3:6
My inner man is being renewed.	2 Cor. 4:16
God gave me the Spirit as a pledge.	2 Cor. 5:5
I am a new creature.	2 Cor. 5:17
God reconciled me to Himself.	2 Cor. 5:18
God is not counting my sins against me.	2 Cor. 5:19
I have become the righteousness of God.	2 Cor. 5:21
God's power is perfected in my weakness.	2 Cor. 12:9
Jesus Christ is in me.	2 Cor. 13:5
God rescued me from this evil age.	Gal. 1:4
I have liberty in Christ Jesus.	Gal. 2:4
I am justified by faith in Christ Jesus.	Gal. 2:16
I died to the Law. I live for God now.	Gal. 2:19
I have been crucified with Christ.	Gal. 2:20
Christ lives in me. I live by faith in Him.	Gal. 2:20
I received the Spirit by hearing with faith.	Gal. 3:2–3
Christ redeemed me from the Law's curse.	Gal. 3:13
I received the promise of the Spirit.	Gal. 3:14
I am not under the Law as a tutor.	Gal. 3:25
I am a child of God through faith.	Gal. 3:26
I was baptized into Christ.	Gal. 3:27
I have been clothed with Christ.	Gal. 3:27
I belong to Christ.	Gal. 3:28
I was adopted as a child of God.	Gal. 4:5
God put the Spirit of His Son in my heart.	Gal. 4:6

I am a child and an heir through God.	Gal. 4:7
I am a child of promise.	Gal. 4:28
Christ set me free.	Gal. 5:1
I have been called to freedom.	Gal. 5:13
My desires agree with the Spirit.	Gal. 5:17
I'm led by the Spirit and not under the Law.	Gal. 5:18
I live by the Spirit and can walk by the Spirit.	Gal. 5:25
I have been crucified to the world.	Gal. 6:14
I walk by the rule of the new creation.	Gal. 6:15–16
I have been blessed with every spiritual blessing.	Eph. 1:3
I am holy and blameless before God.	Eph. 1:4
God kindly adopted me as His child.	Eph. 1:5
God freely bestowed His grace on me.	Eph. 1:6
In Him, I have redemption and forgiveness.	Eph. 1:7
God lavished the riches of His grace on me.	Eph. 1:7–8
I have obtained an inheritance.	Eph. 1:11
I was sealed with the Holy Spirit of promise.	Eph. 1:13
The Spirit is a pledge of my inheritance.	Eph. 1:14
God loved me with His great love.	Eph. 2:4
God made me alive together with Christ.	Eph. 2:5
God raised me and seated me in Heaven in Christ.	Eph. 2:6
I have the gift of salvation by grace through faith.	Eph. 2:8
I am God's workmanship created for good works.	Eph. 2:10
I have been brought near by the blood of Christ.	Eph. 2:13
I have access in the Spirit to the Father.	Eph. 2:18
I am a saint. I am of God's household.	Eph. 2:19
I have bold and confident access to God.	Eph. 3:12
God's power works within me.	Eph. 3:20
I have been called to a new walk.	Eph. 4:1
God's grace has been given to me.	Eph. 4:7
I am growing up in all aspects into Him.	Eph. 4:15
Christ grows me and builds me up in love.	Eph. 4:15–16
I laid aside the old self. I put on the new self.	Eph. 4:22–24

I have been sealed by the Holy Spirit forever.	Eph. 4:30
God has forgiven me in Christ.	Eph. 4:32
Christ loved me and gave Himself up for me.	Eph. 5:2
I am a child of Light.	Eph. 5:8
I am sanctified, cleansed, holy, and blameless.	Eph. 5:26–27
I love Jesus with incorruptible (undying) love.	Eph. 6:24
God began a good work in me and will perfect it.	Phil. 1:6
For me to live is Christ and to die is gain.	Phil. 1:21
God causes me to want and to do as He desires.	Phil. 2:13
I am a blameless and innocent child of God.	Phil. 2:15
I put no confidence in the flesh.	Phil. 3:3
I have righteousness from God.	Phil. 3:9
I am perfect in Christ.	Phil. 3:15
My citizenship is in Heaven.	Phil. 3:20
Christ strengthens me to endure all things.	Phil. 4:13
My God supplies all my needs.	Phil. 4:19
The Father qualified me to share in an inheritance.	Col. 1:12
God rescued me out of darkness.	Col. 1:13
God transferred me to the kingdom of Jesus.	Col. 1:13
I have redemption and forgiveness in Christ.	Col. 1:14
I have been reconciled in Christ's body.	Col. 1:22
I am holy and blameless before God.	Col. 1:22
Christ in me is my hope of glory.	Col. 1:27
God's power works mightily within me.	Col. 1:29
I am now being built up in Christ.	Col. 2:7
I have been made complete in Christ.	Col. 2:10
I was buried and raised with Christ.	Col. 2:12
God made me alive together with Christ.	Col. 2:13
God forgave me of all my sins.	Col. 2:13
God canceled my debt.	Col. 2:14
I died with Christ to the principles of this world.	Col. 2:20
Rules are of no value to me.	Col. 2:21–23
I have been raised up with Christ.	Col. 3:1

My life is hidden with Christ in God.	Col. 3:3
Christ is my life. I will appear with Him in glory.	Col. 3:4
I laid aside the old self with its evil practices.	Col. 3:9
I have put on the new self.	Col. 3:10
I am being renewed to a true knowledge of God.	Col. 3:10
I am chosen of God, holy and beloved.	Col. 3:12
God forgave me (past tense).	Col. 3:13
I will receive the reward of the inheritance.	Col. 3:24
Jesus has rescued me from the wrath to come.	1 Thess. 1:10
God called me into His own kingdom and glory.	1 Thess. 1:12
My heart will be without blame at Christ's return.	1 Thess. 3:13
God has called me for the purpose of purity.	1 Thess. 4:7
I am a child of light and a child of the day.	1 Thess. 5:5
God is faithful to me.	1 Thess. 5:24
I have been called through the Gospel.	2 Thess. 2:14
God has given me eternal comfort and hope.	2 Thess. 2:16
The Lord will protect me from the evil one.	2 Thess. 3:3
The Law is not made for me. I am righteous.	1 Tim. 1:9
Christ Jesus gave Himself as a ransom for me.	1 Tim. 2:6
The Lord gave me a holy calling.	2 Tim. 1:9
The Holy Spirit dwells in me.	2 Tim. 1:13
If I am faithless, Christ still remains faithful.	2 Tim. 2:13
The Lord knows me, and I am His.	2 Tim. 2:19
The Lord will give me a crown of righteousness.	2 Tim. 4:8
God, who cannot lie, promised me eternal life.	Titus 1:2
I am pure, and all things are pure to me.	Titus 1:15
The grace of God teaches me to say "no" to sin.	Titus 2:11–12
God redeemed me and purified me for Himself.	Titus 2:14
God saved me, washed me, and renewed me.	Titus 3:5
God poured out the Holy Spirit upon me richly.	Titus 3:6
I've been justified and made an heir of eternal life.	Titus 3:7
God speaks to me in the message of Jesus.	Heb. 1:2
Jesus purified me of sin once and then sat down.	Heb. 1:3

Jesus is the author of my salvation.	Heb. 2:10
I am sanctified.	Heb. 2:11
Jesus and I have the same Father.	Heb. 2:11
Jesus is not ashamed to call me His sibling.	Heb. 2:11
Jesus comes to my aid when I am tempted.	Heb. 2:18
I am holy and a partaker of a heavenly calling.	Heb. 3:1
I am a partaker of Christ.	Heb. 3:14
I have believed and entered God's rest.	Heb. 4:3
I can draw near with confidence to God's throne.	Heb. 4:16
Jesus is my source of eternal salvation.	Heb. 5:9
Great things accompany my salvation.	Heb. 6:9
Two unchangeables anchor my soul.	Heb. 6:18–19
Jesus entered the Holy Place as a forerunner for me.	Heb. 6:20
The Law is weak, useless, and set aside for me.	Heb. 7:18
I draw near to God through Jesus, my Priest.	Heb. 7:19
Jesus is my guarantee of a new and better covenant.	Heb. 7:22
Jesus saves me forever because He always lives.	Heb. 7:25
God put His laws (desires) in my heart and mind.	Heb. 8:10
I know God intuitively now.	Heb. 8:11
God remembers my sins no more.	Heb. 8:12
The blood of Christ cleansed my conscience.	Heb. 9:14
I received the promise of the eternal inheritance.	Heb. 9:15
Christ suffered once to take away my sins forever.	Heb. 9:26
Christ will return without reference to my sins.	Heb. 9:28
I have been sanctified once and for all.	Heb. 10:10
Christ sat down after taking my sins away.	Heb. 10:12
Christ has perfected me for all time.	Heb. 10:14
The Holy Spirit remembers my sins no more.	Heb. 10:17
I am forgiven and don't need any more sacrifice.	Heb. 10:18
I confidently enter the Holy Place by Jesus's blood.	Heb. 10:19
I can draw near with a sincerity and assurance.	Heb. 10:22
The blood of the covenant sanctified me.	Heb. 10:29
I don't shrink back; I have faith and am preserved.	Heb. 10:39

I please God by faith.	Heb. 11:6
I have something better than Old Testament living.	Heb. 11:40
Jesus is the author and perfecter of my faith.	Heb. 12:2
I am disciplined for my good by my Father.	Heb. 12:7–11
It is good for my heart to be strengthened by grace.	Heb. 13:9
God equips me in every good thing to do His will.	Heb. 13:21
God works in me what is pleasing in His sight.	Heb. 13:21
I will receive the crown of life.	James 1:12
God's Word is implanted in me.	James 1:21
I believe God, and I am His friend.	James 2:23
I am righteous, and my prayer is effective.	James 5:16
I am born again to a living hope.	1 Pet. 1:3
I have an inheritance reserved in Heaven.	1 Pet. 1:4
My salvation is protected by the power of God.	1 Pet. 1:5
My soul is saved.	1 Pet. 1:9
I am a child of obedience.	1 Pet. 1:14
I am redeemed by the blood of Jesus.	1 Pet. 1:18–19
My soul is pure, and I can love from the heart.	1 Pet. 1:22
I am born again of imperishable seed.	1 Pet. 1:23
I am part of a holy priesthood.	1 Pet. 2:5
I am God's own possession.	1 Pet. 2:9
I am an alien and a stranger in this world.	1 Pet. 2:11
I am free as a bondslave of God.	1 Pet. 2:16
I am precious in His sight.	1 Pet. 3:4
I have been given a special gift by God's grace.	1 Pet. 4:10
God cares about me.	1 Pet. 5:7
God perfects, confirms, and strengthens me.	1 Pet. 5:10
I am a partaker of the divine nature.	2 Pet. 1:4
I am purified from sins.	2 Pet. 1:9
I am called and chosen.	2 Pet. 1:10
I am cleansed from all unrighteousness.	1 Jn. 1:9
I have an Advocate with the Father.	1 Jn. 2:1
God's love is perfected in me.	1 Jn. 2:5

My sins are forgiven on account of His name.	1 Jn. 2:12
I have an anointing from God.	1 Jn. 2:20
The Holy Spirit is my Teacher.	1 Jn. 2:27
I am born of Him, and I am righteous.	1 Jn. 2:29
The Father loves me and calls me His child.	1 Jn. 3:1
I am born of God, and I practice righteousness.	1 Jn. 3:9
I have passed from death to life.	1 Jn. 3:14
I have God's Spirit, and I abide in Him.	1 Jn. 3:24
Greater is He who is in me than those in the world.	1 Jn. 4:4
I am from God.	1 Jn. 4:6
I love because I am born of God.	1 Jn. 4:7
I am loved by God, and I live through Him.	1 Jn. 4:9
God abides in me, and His love is perfected in me.	1 Jn. 4:12
I abide in Him, and He abides in me.	1 Jn. 4:13
I can have confidence in the day of judgment.	1 Jn. 4:17
I love because He first loved me.	1 Jn. 4:19
By faith in Him, I have overcome the world.	1 Jn. 5:4–5
I have eternal life, and that life is Jesus.	1 Jn. 5:11–12
God hears my prayers.	1 Jn. 5:14
The evil one cannot touch me.	1 Jn. 5:18
The truth abides in me forever.	2 Jn. 1:2
I have the Father and the Son.	2 Jn. 1:9
I am of God and a doer of good.	3 Jn. 1:11
I am kept for Jesus Christ.	Jude 1:1
I will stand before God, blameless with great joy.	Jude 1:24
I am a priest in God's kingdom.	Rev. 1:6
My name will never be erased from the Book of Life.	Rev. 3:5
I will sit with Jesus on His throne.	Rev. 3:21
I am called, chosen, and faithful.	Rev. 17:14
I am invited to the marriage supper of the Lamb.	Rev. 19:9
I will reign with Him forever.	Rev. 22:5

ADDITIONAL RESOURCES

Get your FREE bonus chapter and discussion questions:

TheGraceMessage.org/book

Are you looking for a church that teaches the grace message?

TheGraceChurch.org

Enjoy other books from Andrew Farley:

The Naked Gospel
God without Religion
Heaven Is Now
The Art of Spiritual War
The Hurt & the Healer
(co-authored with Bart Millard of MercyMe)

Relaxing with God
Twisted Scripture
The Perfect You
(co-authored with Tim Chalas)

Follow Andrew Farley on social media:

Facebook: @DrAndrewFarley
Twitter: @DrAndrewFarley
Instagram: @DrAndrewFarley

Get FREE daily encouragement from The Grace Message with Dr. Andrew Farley:

TheGraceMessage.org